Beres, Samantha.
101 things every kid
should know about science
1998.
33305015159142
CA   01/09/01

101 THINGS EVERY KID SHOULD KNOW ABOUT SCIENCE

By Samantha Beres

Illustrations by Arthur Friedman

LOWELL HOUSE JUVENILE

LOS ANGELES

SANTA CLARA COUNTY LIBRARY

3 3305 01515 9142

To Allison, Sean, Sasha, and Garrett
—S.B.

ACKNOWLEDGMENTS

The author would like to thank Gerald Wheeler of the National Science Teachers Association, Joshua Fischman, editor of *Earth Magazine,* and Annellen Moore, education consultant and science teacher, for adding their expertise to this project.

This title has been reviewed and endorsed by Steve Ingebritsen, hydrogeologist, U.S. Geological Survey; David Lindley, Ph.D.; Sung Chang, New Mexico State University physics department; and Kate Greenly, M.S., genetic counselor, University of Colorado Health Science Center.

Copyright © 1998 by RGA Publishing Group, Inc.
All rights reserved. No part of this work may be reproduced or transmitted in any form or by any means, electronic or mechanical, including photocopying and recording, or by any information storage or retrieval system, except as may be expressly permitted by the 1976 Copyright Act or in writing by the publisher.

Publisher: Jack Artenstein
Director of Publishing Services: Rena Copperman
Editorial Director, Juvenile: Brenda Pope-Ostrow
Director of Juvenile Development: Amy Downing
Designer: S. Pomeroy
Typesetter: Carolyn Wendt

Lowell House books can be purchased at special discounts when ordered in bulk for premiums and special sales. Contact Department CS at the following address:

Lowell House Juvenile
2020 Avenue of the Stars, Suite 300
Los Angeles, CA 90067

Manufactured in the United States of America

10 9 8 7 6 5 4 3 2

Library of Congress Cataloging-in-Publication Data
Beres, Samantha.
  101 things every kid should know about science / by Samantha Beres;
illustrated by Arthur Friedman.
    p. cm.
  Includes index.
  Summary: Presents a variety of facts in such scientific areas as biology, astronomy, and physics.
  ISBN 1-56565-956-2
  1. Science--Miscellanea--Juvenile literature. [1. Science--Miscellanea.]
I. Friedman, Arthur, ill. II. Title.
Q173.B52 1998
500--dc21   97-49847
                                                                  CIP
                                                                  AC

INTRODUCTION
Science Is Everywhere!

You might think of science as a class you have to take in school. Well, it's more than just that! If you haven't realized it already, science is all around you—it happens when you cook something, when it rains outside, or when you cruise down the street on Rollerblades. The list of places and actions that involve science could go on forever.

FROM FAHRENHEIT TO CELSIUS

Subtract 32 from the temperature, multiply the answer by 5, then divide by 9.

Example:
86°F − 32 x 5 ÷ 9 = 30°C

·*101 Things Every Kid Should Know About Science* will give you an overview of many of the different fields of science. While every single aspect of science couldn't be included, we've chosen 101 of the most important science concepts kids your age should be aware of. And we've included a simple table below to convert any of the measurements in this book to the metric system.

We hope that you will use this book as a jumping-off point for discovering the incredible world of science. You may want to do more by researching some of the featured scientists in the Brief Bios, trying some of the Hands On! experiments, or talking to people who work in each field.

Being curious about the world around us is a gift. The best way to use that gift is to search for answers to our questions, and to have fun while doing it.

TO CHANGE IMPERIAL	TO METRIC	MULTIPLY BY
inches	centimeters	2.54
feet	meters	.31
miles	kilometers	1.61
pints	liters	.47
gallons	liters	3.70
ounces	grams	28.35
pounds	kilograms	.045

1 All things are made up of atoms, which are invisible to the eye.

Can you see anything smaller than a flea or a grain of sand? Atoms are much smaller than either of these things. Atoms cannot even be seen with a microscope! Even though we cannot see atoms, all matter is made up of them. Matter is everything around you, from the hair on your head to the sneakers that you're wearing.

Breathe in a lungful of air, or drink a glass of water. Even air and water are made up of atoms! But hair, air, water, and sneakers are four different things, so how could they all be made up of these single things, atoms? Not all atoms are the same. Atoms are like the ingredients

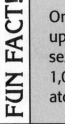

FUN FACT! One drop of water is made up of more than one sextillion atoms (that's 1,000,000,000,000,000,000,000 atoms)!

for a cookie recipe. The ingredients to make peanut butter cookies are different from the ingredients to make chocolate chip cookies. In the same way, atoms that make up air are different from atoms that make up water.

Take, for instance, the matter of water, otherwise known as H_2O. A glass of water is made up of countless water molecules all stuck together. A molecule is a combination of atoms. Each water molecule is made up of two hydrogen atoms (H) and one oxygen atom (O).

2 There are as many different kinds of atoms as there are elements, and there are more than 100 elements in the world.

In ancient times most people believed that everything was made of air, earth, fire, water, or a combination of the four. Now scientists know of 112 elements that are the building blocks of all matter, and there may be more elements that have yet to be discovered. Elements are substances that cannot be broken down into anything simpler. Silver is an element because no matter what you do to it, it is still silver. Silver is made up of silver atoms. Water, on the other

FUN FACT!

Everything in the world is either energy or matter. And energy can change matter. For instance, heat energy can make ice turn to water.

hand, is made up of hydrogen and oxygen atoms. In our everyday lives most of the objects we see are combinations of elements. A few single elements that we do come across are helium (a gas used to fill balloons), gold, aluminum, and copper.

PENCIL LEADS AND DIAMONDS

Carbon is one of the more interesting pure elements. Depending on how the carbon atoms form, it can be pencil lead, charcoal, or diamonds. Each of these things is made up of carbon atoms, but the form that the carbon takes depends on the way the carbon atoms join together.

3 All matter is a gas, a liquid, or a solid.

All things in the world fit into two categories—energy and matter. The matter, which is everything around us, can be a solid, a liquid, or a gas. It depends on how the molecules act.

Here is a way to imagine what goes on in solids, liquids, and gases. Pretend that you and 20 people are in a room, and each one of you is a molecule. If you all pretend that you are part of a solid, like a chunk of plastic, you will stand close together and link arms. You will move back and forth from one foot to another while still touching. Molecules that lock together to make a solid still vibrate (move quickly back and forth), but the movement is so small we don't notice it.

What happens if a solid changes to a liquid? In a liquid, molecules are loosely connected and move more quickly. Imagine this happens to you and the 20 other molecules—you will constantly bump into one another and touch for a second, but will then separate to bump into another person. The molecules in a liquid can slide past one another and do not keep the same neighbors as they do in solids. If a person loses contact with the group and floats out into the room, he or she has become a gas. As gas molecules, you and the group would fill up the whole room and not form a shape. Gas molecules move even faster than those in a liquid. You and the other molecules would run around fast but would hardly ever bump into one another.

FUN FACT! Matter can change form, but matter is never created or destroyed.

A CHANGE OF STATE

When heat or cold changes how the molecules behave, they go through a change of state (which is not driving from Massachusetts to New Hampshire!). For matter, it is a change from a solid to a liquid or a liquid to a gas. A change of state can go the other way, too, from a gas to a liquid or a liquid to a solid.

We see these changes of state clearly with water. When you make ice, the state of water changes from a liquid to a solid. When water boils, the liquid water in the pot changes to steam, a gas.

And if a solid changes to a gas without first being a liquid, it is called sublimation. One way to see sublimation is to take an ice cube out of the freezer. Hold it between your fingers. Some will melt to a liquid on your fingers, but a vapor of steam will also rise off the cube!

4 Rocks, gems, and your teeth are crystals.

A crystal is a type of solid. All solids are made up of atoms that are packed tightly together. In some solids the atoms are locked together in no special order, but the atoms in crystals make a special three-dimensional pattern. This pattern can be squares, triangles, hexagons (six-sided forms), or other shapes with corners, as long as the whole solid is made up of the same repeated pattern. Ice is a crystal. Water atoms lock into hexagonal crystal patterns to form ice. To get a closer look at the corners and flat sides of a crystal, view a single grain of salt, sand, or sugar under a magnifying glass. These are single crystals.

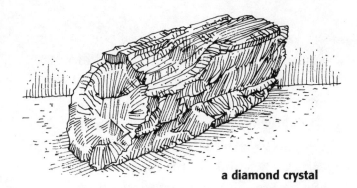

a diamond crystal

HANDS ON!

SEEING CRYSTALS: Illustrate water turning to ice with paper clips. If you lay them on a table in a pile, imagine the pile represents water in liquid form and the paper clips are the water molecules. Take the paper clips and turn them into ice crystals by making hexagons. Make sure that all of the hexagons are right next to each other.

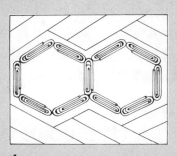

This illustrates water in the form of a solid. Notice how spread out the molecules are and how much space they take up. The same number of molecules (paper clips) are present and still touching, but they are now locked into this crystalline form.

See how the paper clips take up more space?

To read more about crystals, go to pages 35–36.

5 Water is a special substance that we cannot live without.

Water is one of the most important things on Earth. Why? Water is a necessary ingredient for life. About two-thirds of the human body is made of water, and three-fourths of the Earth's surface is water. Fog and clouds are made of water. Water is even in the air we breathe. It's everywhere!

Water is special because it can change to a solid or a gas without difficulty. Think about other substances, like wood and cloth. These things do not easily change. It is important that water can change its form easily, because we also need water vapor and ice to live.

Most substances expand (take up more space) when heated. Water is one of the few substances that expands when frozen. If you fill a glass halfway with water and put it in the freezer, the water level will rise as it freezes. This happens because as the molecules slow down to lock together, they end up farther apart than when they were in liquid form.

6 A change of one kind of matter into another kind of matter is a chemical reaction.

Chemical reactions, which happen around us every day, either give off heat or use up heat. The flame of a gas stove, rust on metal, and baking a cake all happen because of chemical reactions. These things seem very different, but they all have one thing in common: they involve a transfer of energy from heat, light, or electricity to happen. Also, some chemical reactions, such as baking a cake, can't be reversed. Many chemical reactions happen when oxygen atoms meet other atoms. If you turn on a gas stove, a chemical reaction occurs and a flame appears. A natural gas called methane meets with oxygen from the air, and the pilot burner (a constant flame in the stove) provides heat to get the reaction started. The chemical reaction creates a flame.

BRIEF Bio

ANTOINE LAURENT LAVOISIER (1743–1794):
Lavoisier (pronounced luhv-WAH-zee-ay), a French chemist, was the father of modern chemistry. He did many experiments with chemical reactions. Since he accurately measured everything he experimented with, he was able to prove that when materials react with each other and change form, the total amount of matter always stays the same. He also showed that no material will burn without oxygen. Because of Lavoisier, scientists who came after him were able to understand that air is not just one gas but a blend of gaseous elements. Later in his life he wrote a book that provided a definition for the elements that is still used today: "All substances which we have not yet been able by any means to decompose are elements to us."

THE ALCHEMISTS

Long before any of the elements were known, scientists in the Middle Ages, called alchemists, experimented with metals. They tried to change base metals such as lead into gold. Even though the alchemists were unsuccessful, they did discover some elements. They also used procedures that chemists still use in laboratories today. Most important, though, the alchemists were the first to observe and experiment with chemical reactions, changing one kind of matter into another.

7 | All matter has mass and density.

Mass is the amount of material something is made of. Density compares the mass of two things with the same volume. For instance, a cup of water has more mass than a cup of vegetable oil, even though they are both one cup. The water is more dense than the vegetable oil, which is why oil floats on water. Compare the density of two things that are the same size in dimension, say a marble and a chunk of cookie dough exactly the same size. The marble is a lot heavier (and has more mass) even though it is the same size. This means that the marble is more dense than the cookie dough. Now compare two things that are the same weight, like a pound of lead and a pound of feathers. They both weigh the same, but the feathers take up a lot more space! The pound of feathers is *less* dense than the lead.

EUREKA! IN THE BATHTUB

Archimedes (pronounced ar-kuh-MEE-deez) is famous for exclaiming, "Eureka!" (I have found it!). Archimedes was the chief scientist for King Hieron of Syracuse (now Sicily, Italy). The king asked Archimedes to prove that his crown was made of pure gold. The king was very suspicious that silver was hidden under the gold surface. Archimedes had to prove or disprove it without destroying the beautiful crown.

HANDS ON!

DENSITY IN THE KITCHEN SINK: Experiment with density right in your own kitchen sink! Fill it with water and put small objects into it to see what is more or less dense than water. If something floats, it is less dense; if it sinks, it is more dense. Try pennies, marbles, ice, balls of foil, or anything else around the house, as long as your parents say it is okay. What do you find out?

While sitting in the bathtub, he realized that the water in the tub rises when something is put into it: the bigger the object, the more the water rises. So he made a solid gold block weighing exactly the same as the king's crown. If the crown were really pure gold, it would have exactly the same volume as the gold block. But if the crown had some less dense material such as silver inside it, it would have to be bigger than the gold block in order to weigh the same.

When he put the gold block in and the water did not rise as high as it did when the crown was dunked, he proved that the crown was made of something less dense than gold!

8 Energy can never be destroyed—it is constantly in use or being stored for future use.

Energy is mysterious. We eat food for energy, we save energy by turning off unneeded lights, and we buy batteries, which store energy, for our radios, cameras, and Walkmans. We know what it does, but we cannot see it. We also know that energy moves from one thing to another.

Food, for example, is energy that fuels your body. When you eat, chemical reactions in your body convert energy in the food into energy for you. Calories listed on food packages say how much energy is in the food. We burn calories all the time, even when we are sleeping. If you go out to play baseball, you need more energy than you do when you're sleeping, because you are burning more calories. When you do something, such as throw a ball, energy moves from your body to the ball.

All of these actions take energy, which comes from the food you eat. But where does the food come from? Some of our food comes from plants, which store energy from the sun. Energy is constantly being recycled and just keeps getting passed around!

9 Kinetic energy and potential energy are two important forms of energy.

Energy that can be stored and used later is called potential energy. For instance, if a dam is holding back water, the water has potential energy. When the dam is let down, the energy is set free, shown in flowing water. This is called kinetic energy. Another example of potential and kinetic energy can be found in springs. When a spring is pushed in, it has potential energy, and when it springs out, it uses kinetic energy.

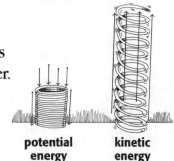

potential energy   **kinetic energy**

You would be surprised how many things around your house store potential energy in springs, such as pens (with clickers on the top), scales, spray bottles, and staplers. Can you figure out how springs help these objects work?

10 Heat is energy that flows from warmer objects to colder ones.

"Close the door! You're letting all of the heat out!" Your mom or dad might holler this during winter months if you're holding the door open for too long. If heat didn't travel so much, we wouldn't have to insulate our houses to hold heat in because the heat would just stay there.

Heat moves around a lot and always does the same thing—it constantly moves to a cooler place, until the temperature evens out. If you have a hot drink, it cools off and eventually ends up at room temperature because the temperature has evened out.

HANDS ON!

FIND A GOOD CONDUCTOR: Conduction occurs when heat travels through something, usually a solid. To see conduction in action, try this. Put a wooden spoon and a metal spoon in a hot drink. After a minute, feel each one. What happens? When you put a metal spoon in hot liquid, it gets hot, fast. That's because metal is a good conductor, and the heat travels from the drink into the spoon easily. Wood is not a good conductor, so the wooden spoon in a hot drink doesn't get hot. Experiment with other materials.

11 If it weren't for the Earth's invisible force of gravity, we would float off into space!

All objects pull on each other with a force called gravitation. That means that everything in your bathroom—the sink, bathtub, towels, even soap—is pulling on each other slightly. We don't notice the pulls between all of the things around us because there is such a big pull from the Earth, holding everything down. The bigger the mass of something, the stronger the pull. Because the Earth is so huge, it has a much stronger pull than little objects such as towels and bathtubs. This is why, when a ball falls to the ground, we notice the Earth's gravitational pull on the ball without realizing that the ball is pulling on the Earth, too!

BRIEF Bio

ALBERT EINSTEIN (1879–1955): Albert Einstein, from Germany, was one of the greatest scientists ever. He is known for his theory of relativity. From this theory, he came up with the equation energy equals mass times the speed of light squared, or $E=mc^2$. It proves that mass can be changed into energy and that energy can be changed into mass.

Weight is a measure of gravitational pull. The moon is much smaller than the Earth and so is its gravitational pull. This is why astronauts can jump high when they visit the moon. They weigh much less than they do here on Earth, but their mass has not changed at all. If you went to the moon, your mass would stay the same, too, but you would weigh six times less because the gravitational pull on the moon is not as strong as it is on Earth.

HANDS ON!

THE WEIGHT OF AIR: Air has mass, and there is gravity on Earth, so it must weigh something! Make your own scale by tying a string to the center of a ruler or a stick. Hang an empty balloon off each end using string. When you hold on to the center string, the stick should be straight across (horizontal). Now take one of the balloons off and blow it up. Hang it back on the stick. What happens?

12 | Electricity can create a force.

Electricity, like gravity, pushes and pulls things and therefore is a force. Take static electricity, for example. If you rub a balloon on your head, you can stick the balloon to a wall. Actually, it pulls to the wall. This happens because of an imbalance in atoms. Atoms are too tiny to see even with a microscope and are made up of things even smaller. In every atom are protons, which are positively charged, and electrons, which are negatively charged. Electricity happens because of the negative electrons. Usually each atom balances out with positive and negative charges. If electrons and protons are separated, an imbalance occurs, causing electricity.

an atom

So what happens when you rub a balloon on your hair? Some negatively charged electrons move or jump from your hair to the balloon. The balloon then has an overall negative charge. Put the balloon near a wall. Since it is negatively charged, it first repels other negative charges (electrons) on the wall. It pushes them away. Then that part of the wall is positively charged while the balloon is still negatively charged. Positives and negatives attract, so the balloon sticks to the wall. The balloon falls off the wall when all of the atoms have evened out again.

Current electricity is static electricity in motion. It occurs when electrons travel, trying to get away from a place that has a negative force (too many electrons) to a place with a positive force (not enough electrons). For instance, if a battery powers something, there is a negative and a positive side of the battery. The electrons leave the negative side through a wire. They are attracted to the positive side to even the sides out. As the electrons move back to the battery, they flow through the wire and power whatever is at the end of the wire before traveling back.

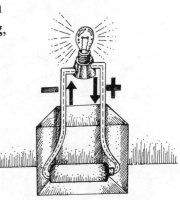

See pages 4–5 to read more about atoms.

13 A compass uses a magnetic force to tell you which way is north.

Have you ever wondered how the arrow on a compass can always face north? It has to do with magnetic forces. Magnetic force is a natural force (push or pull) just like gravity. It's the force that makes magnets pull to the refrigerator or pick up a nail. If you hold two magnets together, they will pull together, or they will push apart. Both the push and the pull are magnetic forces.

unlike poles attract each other

like poles push away from each other

Individual atoms are often magnetic. If the atomic magnets are distributed randomly, the object is not magnetic. If the atomic magnets are lined up and the positive forces all face one way, the negative forces face the other way. Then the object is magnetic.

In every magnet there is a north pole and a south pole. If you hold two magnets near each other and they pull together, one end is a north pole and the other

FUN FACT!

Magnetite is a rock that is a natural magnet. It was first found in a place called Magnesia, a port city in Greece, which is where the word *magnet* comes from.

HANDS ON!

MAKE A MAGNET: You'll need an iron nail, a paper clip, and a magnet. Take one pole of the magnet and rub it from top to bottom along the nail. Keep rubbing the nail only from top to bottom—rubbing back and forth both ways won't work. After several rubs, you should be able to pick up the paper clip with the nail because all of the negative charges in the nail will be pointing in the same direction.

end is a south pole. If two north poles, or two south poles, are put together, they will repel, or push away from, each other.

Earth itself is like an enormous magnet. Its North Pole and South Pole act as opposite ends of a magnet. The little arrow on the compass can always point north because it is a magnet that lines its north pole up with the Earth's North Pole.

14 Friction is a force that slows things down.

Friction is the force that acts against or resists movement. You use friction when you put the brakes on while riding a bike. The brake rubs on the wheel, creates friction, and stops the movement of the wheel. An object slows down depending on how much friction it comes across. If you were to go sledding down a grassy hill in the summer, there would be so much friction between the sled and the ground that you probably wouldn't get too far. However, when there is snow or ice on the ground, there is less friction between the sled and the snow, and you would travel much farther than you did on the grassy slope.

15 Newton's first law of motion: A body in motion tends to remain in motion.

That is, something in motion will move in a straight line at the same speed forever unless another force changes it. It may seem impossible that an object, like a ball thrown into the air, could move in a straight line forever. It would, though, if it weren't for some other forces acting on it, such as gravity, which pulls the ball toward the ground. Friction, caused by air, also slows the ball down. And if someone catches it, then his or her hands act as another force to stop the ball's motion.

Sometimes you are the "object" that wants to keep moving in a straight line. If you stand in the aisle of a moving bus, you and the bus are heading down the street at the same speed. But when the bus stops, your body jolts forward because it wants to keep going. Fortunately, you can hold on to something and you will stop; otherwise,

BRIEF Bio

ISAAC NEWTON (1642–1727):
Imagine the motion of absolutely anything, from a comet screaming through the sky to the waves in the ocean to you just walking across a room. Sir Isaac Newton, a famous scientist, came up with the three laws of motion that explain all motion in the universe! Newton was born in England and spent his life there. He went to Cambridge University, and after graduating, he published works describing the nature of color and light. Newton also invented calculus. In 1705 Queen Anne made Newton a knight. He was the first scientist to receive this honor.

you'd fly right out of the bus! (See the importance of seat belts in cars?)

Newton's first law also says that something at rest will stay at rest unless another force acts on it. If the bus is at a complete stop, you and the bus are "at rest." When the bus takes off, your body wants to stay "at rest." This is why you jerk back in your seat if the driver takes off really fast. What is happening is that the bus seat is moving into your back and your body is trying to stay right where it is!

16 Newton's second law: Force equals mass times acceleration.

Newton's second law states that the greater the force applied to an object, the faster it speeds up; the bigger and heavier the object, the more force is needed to move it. If you kick a ball, your foot puts force on the ball to make it move. When you kick harder, you are applying a "greater force" so that the ball can go faster. Newton's second law also says that the more mass an object has, the more force you'll need to move it. It will take more force to kick a soccer ball across a field than it will a smaller, lighter ball. Or, if you think of lifting things, you know it takes more force to lift a stack of books than a pillow. (The stack of books has more mass than the pillow.)

17 Newton's third law: For every action there is an opposite and equal reaction.

You can see Newton's third law in many ways. When you hit a baseball with a bat, the bat pushes on the ball and sends the ball into the distance. This is the action. The reaction is the ball pushing on the bat. That's why you feel a jolt in your arms and shoulders when you make a big hit!

Some actions and reactions aren't so obvious. When you eat dinner, your plate pushes down on the table. Not only that, but the table pushes up on the plate with an equal push! The plate pushing down is an action, the table pushing up is a reaction. Sound like a weird action and reaction? Imagine if the table didn't push up on the plate with an equal push. You would set the table at night, and the table would start sinking!

18 The speed of sound through air is 343 meters per second.

When you open your mouth to speak, the sound of your voice travels to get to the listener's ear. It travels so fast that you don't even think about the air that the sound travels through! All sounds start with a vibration. When you talk, your vocal chords move back and forth quickly, or vibrate. If you put your hands on your throat while talking, you can feel these vibrations.

Your moving vocal chords vibrate the molecules around them. These air molecules push all the other air molecules around them, causing them to vibrate, too.

THE SPEED OF SOUND

The denser the molecules of an object, the faster sound will travel through it.

Sound travels at:	In what material?
1,402 meters per second	through water
1,522 meters per second	in sea water
6,420 meters per second	through aluminum

The molecules vibrating against each other make the sound waves that reach your ears.

Sound waves sometimes bounce off hard surfaces to make echoes. These waves can break glass if the waves traveling through the air are a certain length. These waves can make a sonic boom—a really loud noise— if an object such as a fighter jet is going faster than the speed of sound! (Most nonmilitary planes fly slower than 343 meters per second to avoid making sonic booms.)

We often hear sound that travels through the air, but sound waves also travel through solids and liquids. Next time you are swimming or in the bathtub, go under water to hear sounds. Sound travels faster through solid things than it does through air, because the molecules in solid things are packed more tightly together. So the closer the molecules, the faster the sound will go!

HANDS ON!

GOOD VIBRATIONS: Try this observation with a rubber band. Stretch the rubber band out on one hand between two fingers. Pluck it with your other hand, then let it go quickly so that it vibrates. Hear the sound? When does the sound stop? Now hook the rubber band on one of your teeth and stretch it out away from your mouth. (Don't stretch it too much!) Pluck it again. It will sound louder this time because it's traveling through a solid—your tooth and jaw—to get to your ear!

19 Light travels at 186,282 miles (about 300 million meters) per second.

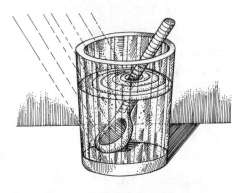

If you could move as fast as light waves travel, you could run around the Earth about eight times in a second! When sunlight hits the Earth, or when you turn on a light, the light travels in a constant stream of energy waves. Have you ever put a spoon in a glass of water? If you look through the side of the glass, the spoon appears to bend where it meets the water. Of course, it doesn't really bend, but why does it look that way? When light waves travel through the air and hit the water, they slow down, causing the waves to bend. When the light refracts, or bends, an illusion of a bending spoon is created.

20 White light is made up of the seven colors of the rainbow.

When you mix red, orange, yellow, green, blue, indigo, and violet *lights,* you see white light. The seven colors of light travel in waves. When the light waves hit something like falling raindrops, or a prism, the colors' waves bend at different angles, creating a rainbow.

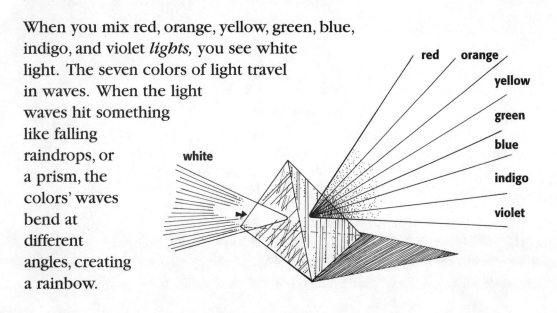

HANDS ON!

MAKE A RAINBOW: To make your own rainbow, ask an adult if you can use a hose or a sprinkler. If you can spray the hose or the sprinkler in exactly the right place to catch the light waves from the sun, you'll see a rainbow! Face the sun when spraying and make sure the water is coming out as a thin spray of water into the air. You may have to move it around until you find just the right angle to make your very own rainbow. *Never look directly into the sun—you can permanently damage your eyes.*

Two important sources of energy are the sun, a renewable resource, and fossil fuels, which are nonrenewable.

Sun, water, and wind are all renewable resources for energy. *Renewable* means that they don't get used up. We never have to worry about running out of these energy sources, but we must come up with ways to harness or capture this energy. The sun gives us solar energy in the form of heat and light rays. The sun shining through windows to warm up a room is one example of solar energy. People have created solar panels to collect the sun's energy, windmills to capture energy from the wind, and hydropower plants to harness water for power.

Fossil fuel resources are more commonly used for energy and are nonrenewable, which means they cannot be replaced

WHERE DO FOSSIL FUELS COME FROM?

Fossil fuels are formed from buried dead animals and plants. For example, coal is formed from plants. First, the plants die and turn into peat, which has the texture of a very light dirt or soil and is rich in organic carbon from the disintegrated plants. Over millions of years heat and pressure deep underground turn the peat into coal. Ninety percent of the energy used in the United States comes from fossil fuels.

quickly. These nonrenewable resources include coal, oil, and natural gas. The resources come from underground and take millions of years to form. We are using them up much faster than they are made! And, unlike sun, water, and wind sources, burning fossil fuels creates a lot of pollution.

22 An ecosystem is a community of living and nonliving things in one area.

In any given area, plants, animals, rocks, sand, and other living and nonliving things interact with each other. Ecologists call these ecosystems. An ecosystem can be a desert, a jungle, a forest, or a pond. It could also be a city block or a small neighborhood park. Each ecosystem is its own patch of land, and the world is made up of these patches. Every part of an ecosystem, right down to the bacteria in the soil, is important to the whole system. Many ecosystems are stable, meaning that plants and animals can survive in the system for a long while. If there is a disturbance, such as a shortage of water or food, the life-forms in the ecosystem start to die and the system becomes unstable. Other disturbances may be caused by fires, droughts, or building developments.

23 Three kinds of rocks make up most of the Earth's crust: igneous, sedimentary, and metamorphic.

Even though when we look at the ground, we may see roads, houses, trees, and dirt, most of the Earth is made up of rock. But what are rocks made of and how are they formed? It depends on the rock! Some sedimentary rocks start on the surface of the Earth when sand, soil, and pebbles are worn down by water and weather. The sediment (pieces of sand, soil, and pebbles) is washed into rivers, lakes, and oceans, where it piles up. As pressure increases, this sediment molds together to form layered-looking rocks. Many other sedimentary rocks begin beneath the oceans, for example, as coral reefs. Igneous rocks, on the other hand, come from hot liquid magma deep in the Earth. As magma nears the surface, it cools to form such rocks as granite. Metamorphic rocks are formed deep underground, where pressure and heat cause igneous and sedimentary rocks to change their form or "metamorphose." Rocks are in a continual cycle. As they move about the Earth over time by erosion or tectonic plate movements, they change form. For instance, a rock formed at the surface may work its way underground and, over time, become a metamorphic rock.

WHAT'S THE DIFFERENCE BETWEEN ROCKS AND MINERALS?

Rocks are combinations of minerals. Minerals, on the other hand, are made up entirely of a single element or a compound of elements and have a particular crystalline form. Some minerals that are one element are diamonds, gold, and silver. Not all elements are minerals. A mineral must be an element that takes on a certain crystalline form.

Turn to pages 4–5, 9, 24, and 53 to read about the elements.

24 | The center of the Earth is metal and is at least 6,700° Fahrenheit.

If you look at a hard-boiled egg and its three main parts, you get an idea of the layers of the Earth. No one has ever gone to the center of the Earth, but scientists have ideas about what it is made of from studying the Earth's density and the way that seismic waves pass through it. The center of the Earth has a core, much like a yolk. At the very center is a solid inner core made of iron and nickel metals. It is very hot, but there is so much pressure at the center of the Earth that it cannot melt. The outer core is also iron and nickel and is molten metal,

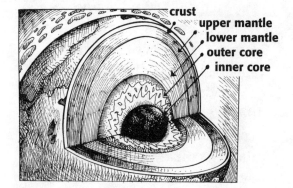

crust
upper mantle
lower mantle
outer core
inner core

like a thick pudding. Made of hot rock, the mantle is about 1,800 miles thick and is similar to the egg white. The crust of the Earth, which lies on the mantle, can be compared to the egg shell. This crust is anywhere from 4 to 43 miles deep, but compared to the rest of Earth, it is a thin layer and is made up of igneous, sedimentary, and metamorphic rocks.

INGREDIENTS TO "MAKE AN EARTH"

The Earth is made of close to 100 different elements, but most of the Earth is made of the elements silicon, oxygen, aluminum, iron, calcium, sodium, potassium, and magnesium. The surface of the Earth is mostly oxygen and silicon. Silicon is one of the ingredients in sand, glass, and computer chips.

25 | All of the continents were once connected in one huge continent now known as Pangaea.

The seven continents were not always separated as they are today. Approximately 200 million years ago the world's continents were one huge piece of land. The name for this supercontinent is Pangaea. If you think of Pangaea as a puzzle, you can imagine the puzzle splitting in half, as Pangaea did 180 million years ago. Then, 65 million years ago, the two large continents broke into the smaller ones we have today.

Widely accepted by scientists, the theory of plate tectonics, or continental drift, states that there are many moving plates underneath the continents and

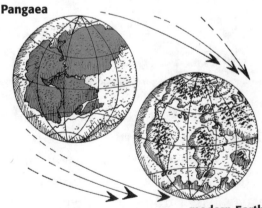

Pangaea

modern Earth

FUN FACT! Eurasia and North America move at least an inch away from each other every year. Africa and South America move about 1½ inches away from each other every year.

the oceans. These plates are like the pieces of the puzzle that were once connected. Each plate is an enormous piece of rock about 60 miles thick made up of the Earth's crust and part of the mantle. These 12 large plates and a number of smaller ones don't line up exactly with the continents that we live on. They are in constant motion, and so the continents ride on the plates and move little by little. The plates are in motion because they slide on a partly molten (hot liquid rock) layer of the mantle.

BRIEF Bio

ALFRED WEGENER (1880–1930):
Wegener was a German meteorologist. He first proposed the idea of continental drift. He also believed that all of the land on the Earth's crust was once a supercontinent, now known as Pangaea. Few believed Wegener at the time. He did have proof of rock formations on opposite sides of the Atlantic that matched up; however, he did not have a convincing explanation for how the continents moved. Now scientists have proof of moving continents, and Wegener's theories are widely accepted.

Turn to pages 23–24 to read about the layers of the Earth.

26 A volcano is a hole or a crack in the crust of the Earth that lava and ash come out of.

Volcanoes are often pictured as large cone-shaped mountains that spit out tons of flowing lava from the top. Some volcanoes do look like this, but there are other volcanoes that are nothing more than long cracks in the ground that ooze lava. Some volcanoes are dead, meaning they don't erupt anymore and are not expected to erupt in the future. If a volcano is fuming—letting out smoke, oozing, or erupting—it is "active." A volcano is considered "alive" if it's expected to erupt sometime in the future.

Volcanoes erupt because of heat and pressure underground. Magma (liquid rock) is as far as 90 miles below the Earth's surface. Blobs of hot liquid magma and gas are less dense than the surrounding rock so that they start to move upward. As gas moves toward the surface, it expands and looks for a place to escape. The gas finds its way to the surface of Earth through a vent and brings hot molten rock with it. When magma reaches the air, it is called lava. Sometimes volcanoes just ooze slowly, but other times an explosion shoots the hot red rock high into the air! The "smoke" that fills the sky during and after a volcanic eruption is a thick cloud of ash.

THE RING OF FIRE

The Ring of Fire is a circle of volcanoes in a region in the Pacific Ocean, from South America to Alaska to Japan, Indonesia, and New Zealand. Of the 850 active volcanoes in the world, over 75 percent are in this Ring of Fire. (This area is also prone to earthquakes!)

27 An intricate web of water flows through openings under the Earth's surface.

If you were to pour water over a bucket of sand and watch it make its way through tiny nooks and crannies, you could get an idea of how water in the Earth's underground water system moves. Not all groundwater stays underground, though. Some groundwater reaches the surface to form springs.

When groundwater is heated by hot rock, it expands and rises. Sometimes this groundwater reaches the surface to form hot springs, bubbling pools of hot water on the surface of the land. In the case of geysers, hot water gathers in a chamber

FUN FACT!

Some geysers can shoot water over 200 feet into the air!

underground with steam and gas. As the steam expands, there is pressure buildup, and the water erupts by spraying into the air.

ENERGY FROM UNDERGROUND

Geothermal energy uses the Earth's natural heat by tapping into hot water underground. Some water gets to be 751° Fahrenheit! The hot water can't boil because it's trapped in rock at high pressure, but it can provide steam that can move turbines—big wheels that turn—to power generators. In Iceland whole towns are powered by geothermal energy.

Over 800,000 earthquakes happen around the world each year.

Although thousands of earthquakes occur every year, only 20 or 30 are large enough to be destructive enough to hurt people and damage buildings. Most earthquakes are not felt at all and are only recorded by instruments, which are read by scientists.

Earthquakes happen when enormous pieces of rock below the surface of Earth push past each other or slide over one another. When stress builds up, the rocks

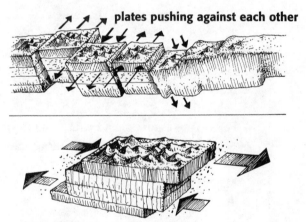

plates pushing against each other

plates sliding over one another

THE BIGGEST SHOCKER IN THE STATES

One of the most severe earthquakes in the United States took place in New Madrid, Missouri. The series of quakes started in December 1811 and lasted until March 1812. The quakes were felt all over the states and in Canada and consisted of three major shocks and thousands of aftershocks. The land was changed so much that the course of the Mississippi River was changed and new lakes were created!

may shift suddenly or break. This sends wave vibrations upward to the surface, making the ground tremble. Sometimes a quake lasts only a few minutes, but aftershocks can happen for days, even weeks, afterward. Aftershocks are ground tremors that occur after the initial quake. They are caused by wave vibrations, too.

Earthquakes are measured by two different scales, the Mercalli scale and the Richter scale.

THE RICHTER SCALE

The Richter scale uses a machine called a seismograph to measure the ground waves at the source of an earthquake. It goes up to 8.9.

1. Detectable by instruments only.
2. Barely felt.
3. Felt indoors.
4. Felt by most people and causes slight damage.
5. Felt by everyone and causes minor damage.
6. Moderately destructive.
7. Major damage.
8. Total and major damage.

MERCALLI SCALE

The Mercalli has 12 points and measures the damage an earthquake creates.

1. Is not felt.
2. Felt by people in upper stories.
3. Hanging objects swing.
4. Windows and doors rattle.
5. People sleeping are awakened.
6. Books fall off shelves.
7. Chimneys fall, mud banks collapse.
8. Houses are damaged, ground cracks.
9. Serious damage to buildings and underground pipes.
10. Most buildings destroyed.
11. Railroad lines bent.
12. Total destruction, objects thrown into air.

DESTRUCTIVE EARTHQUAKES

Date	Place	Damage
1556	China	more than 800,000 people killed
1906	San Francisco, CA	452 people killed; about $500 million damage
1923	Japan	more than 575,000 houses destroyed
1988	Armenia	more than 25,000 people killed

29 Mountains are continually growing or shrinking.

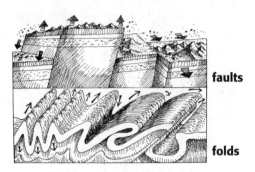

faults

folds

Some mountains are young and some are old. How old they are depends on when they started. Mountains and hills begin growing when movements of the Earth's tectonic plates form either a fault or a fold. When the rocks are under strain and crack, or fracture, they form a fault. When the rock crumples and pushes the land upward, a fold is formed.

Fault-block mountains form when a whole block of land rises upward between two faults. Fold mountains grow when rock bends into folds. The valleys are shaped by streams. Mountains also form when volcanoes erupt, such as Mauna Kea, one of the tallest mountains in the world. Mauna Kea started at the bottom of the ocean floor and kept oozing lava year after year, until finally it rose above sea level. Now, even though it is more than 33,000 feet high, only about 13,700 feet of it is above sea level. Mount Everest, the highest point of land in the world, is a mountain 29,028 feet above sea level.

FUN FACT!

The Himalayan mountain range in Asia contains 20 of the highest mountains in the world. They began to form when India collided with Asia 40 million years ago.

Go to pages 24–25 to read about plate tectonics.

30 Glaciers are long, moving rivers of ice that move about 1 foot a week.

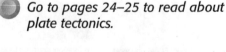

About 96 percent of the Earth's glaciers are in Antarctica and Greenland. Glaciers form because of gradual accumulation of snow, which, when squeezed together, becomes layers of ice. If you take a snowball and squeeze it really hard, it can become hard and icy, because the warmth of your hand melts it and the pressure of your squeeze pushes it together to refreeze as ice. This is similar to how glaciers form. In the mountains are snowfields covered with heavy snow.

The snow is so heavy that it presses down on the snow below it. As more snow falls and more pressure is applied, the snow changes form and compresses into ice, building huge layers of glacier ice.

FUN FACT!

Only 25 percent of the world is covered with land. About 10.4 percent of the land is covered with ice.

Glaciers are so large and heavy— some as thick as 3 miles!—that they carve out valleys as they move. Glaciers that move as one big hunk of ice are called warm-based glaciers. Cold-based glaciers move differently. The top layer of ice slides over the bottom layer. Most glaciers are a combination of both movements.

31 All rivers start from a source, such as mountain springs or melting glaciers.

Rivers come in all shapes and sizes. Some rivers flow only right after it rains. The smallest rivers are called rills. Other small rivers are called streams and brooks.

Rivers are sculptors of the Earth because they change the shape of the land through erosion (wearing away). Over long periods of time rivers can even make a

FUN FACT!

The Colorado River took 15 million years to carve out the Grand Canyon. The Grand Canyon is 217 miles long and the largest gorge in the world—4 to 13 miles wide and 4,000 to 5,500 feet deep.

canyon. When a river erodes the land, the running water carries materials (silt, sand, and gravel) downstream and deposits them somewhere else. Most rivers run into another body of water, such as a lake or an ocean. Between the river and the body of water is a river's delta. In the delta the river slows and drops a lot of the material it has been carrying. Sand bars, swamps, and lagoons are also found in the delta.

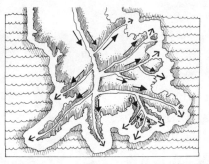

A river with many branches leading to a large body of water. Can you find the deltas?

FUN FACT! The longest river in the world is the Nile in Africa at 4,160 miles.

32 Most of the ocean floor is more than 6,560 feet deep.

Just as there is landscape on Earth's land, the ocean bed also has a landscape. The "bed" is another name for the floor of the ocean, which, like land, includes mountains, hills, canyons, and valleys. In general, the ocean bed near the continents could be thought of as a sort of slide, called the

FUN FACT! The lowest point of the ocean is the bottom of the Marianas Trench in the Pacific Ocean. The trench is nearly 7 miles deep!

continental margin, that is shallow, steep, and then shallow again. Starting at the shoreline is a shallow slope called the continental shelf. Then the slide gets really steep. This steep part of the ocean floor is the continental slope, and it goes down to the bottom of the ocean. A gentle angle between this steep slope and the floor is the continental rise.

33 Currents, waves, and tides keep the ocean waters in constant motion.

At the beach we see waves crashing on the shore and the tide slowly working its way in and out between high tide and low tide. And currents that are not as visible to the eye happen throughout the ocean waters. How does the ocean make all of these movements?

Waves and currents on the upper ocean waters are made by wind. Waves start out as little ripples; then the ripple catches wind and gets bigger. Because it is growing, the ripple can catch more wind, getting even bigger and turning into a wave.

If you have ever seen the

ocean currents (The arrows indicate the directions in which the waters move.)

human wave at a ball game, you noticed that people take turns standing to create the wave, but they never move from their seats. This is how ocean waves work. Energy moves through the water, and the water goes up and down rather than forward, even though it looks as if it is going forward.

Surface currents happen in the top 300 feet of ocean water. These currents do not flow in straight lines but are pulled into curves by the Corrolis effect, which is caused by the rotation of the Earth. The currents in the deep ocean waters often move in the opposite direction from the surface currents and are caused by temperature changes. Cold water is denser (heavier) than warm water, and it sinks to the bottom. These cold waters move slowly toward warmer waters of the Earth.

Wind and temperature changes create waves and currents to keep the water constantly moving, but tides move for a completely different reason. The tides depend on how the Earth and moon are facing each other. As the Earth turns on its axis, the moon travels around the Earth. The Earth and the moon both "pull" on one another because of gravity. We cannot notice this pull, but the ocean water, which is like a big blanket on the Earth, is pulled by the moon's gravity. The oceans on the Earth that directly face the moon are pulled more, creating a "bulge" of water along the shores on that

DON'T CATCH THIS WAVE

Tsunamis are gigantic waves that happen after an earthquake on the ocean floor. They can travel up to 435 miles per hour and can be up to 100 feet tall!

side, called high tide. On the other side of the Earth, the oceans not facing the moon are at low tide. As the Earth turns and the moon moves, the place on Earth where the pull is stronger changes, so the tides change, too. The time between the high and low tides is a little different from place to place, but the ocean rises as high tide twice a day.

Our atmosphere, several layers of gases that wrap around the Earth, is about 430 miles deep.

The Earth's atmosphere is divided into layers. Each layer blends into another, but the temperature in one is extremely different from that in the next.

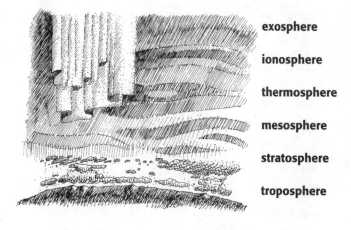

exosphere

ionosphere

thermosphere

mesosphere

stratosphere

troposphere

We live in the troposphere. It extends 5 to 11 miles above the ground, depending on what part of the Earth you're on. The troposphere holds most of the water vapor in the atmosphere and is where all of our weather takes place. The upper part of this layer can get as cold as -67°F.

The stratosphere is about 30 miles thick. The ozone layer, which protects

WHY IS THE OZONE LAYER SO IMPORTANT?

Each air molecule in the ozone layer absorbs dangerous ultraviolet rays from the sun. If it weren't for the ozone layer, the ultraviolet rays would reach Earth and we'd burn up. One chemical, chlorofluorocarbons (CFCs), can eat holes in the ozone layer, allowing ultraviolet rays to pass through to the Earth. That's why it's important not to let too many CFCs into the air. CFCs come from coolant in air conditioners, some insulation, mattresses, and Styrofoam cups.

us from the sun's ultraviolet rays, is in the stratosphere. The temperature in this layer is usually around 28°F.

The ionosphere has two parts. The mesosphere is the lower part and the temperatures can get to a freezing -184°F. The air is thinner than the air below but is thick enough to slow things down (like meteors flying through the air). The higher part of the ionosphere, the thermosphere, is a hot 3,600°F because it absorbs ultraviolet light from the sun.

The highest layer is the exosphere, where the gas thins as it merges with outer space.

35 When air is warmed by land and water, it rises and causes wind, hurricanes, cyclones, and tornadoes.

Hot air rises and cold air sinks, and as the air moves around, wind is created. The sun heats up bodies of land and water, which in turn warm up the air.

Hurricanes (sometimes called typhoons), cyclones, and tornadoes start when air warms quickly and rises. Cool air then rushes underneath, causing the air to spiral. Hurricanes and cyclones often start over the ocean. Cyclones can spin from 10 to 60 miles per hour and travel a distance of about 25 miles per hour. A hurricane is a tropical cyclone that can spin from 75 to 200 miles per hour and travel a distance of 10 to 20 miles per hour. Cyclones and hurricanes can cause a great deal of damage to the coastline but tend to die down as soon as they hit land.

Tornadoes start the same way, but over land, and have winds that spin up to 300 miles per hour. They travel from 25 to 40 miles an hour and usually last only minutes.

WHAT IS THE WINDCHILL FACTOR?

Wind, depending on how fast it is moving, makes the air feel colder than it actually is. The windchill factor describes this feeling. For example, it may be 30°F outside. If the wind isn't blowing, the windchill temperature will be 30°F, too, but if the wind starts to howl, the windchill temperature goes down!

THE FUJITA-PEARSON SCALE

The Fujita-Pearson scale is used to measure tornadoes by their wind speed. The scale is named for Dr. Theodore Fujita and Allen Pearson, who designed the scale. Most tornadoes are an F0 or an F1.

type	wind speed	damage	damage description
F0	40–72 mph	light	damage to trees, billboards, and chimneys
F1	72–112 mph	moderate	mobile homes pushed off their foundations, cars pushed off roads
F2	113–157 mph	considerable	roofs torn off, mobile homes demolished, and large trees uprooted
F3	158–206 mph	severe	homes torn apart, trees uprooted, and cars lifted off the ground
F4	207–260 mph	devastating	houses leveled, cars thrown, objects become flying missiles
F5	261+ mph	incredible	structures lifted off foundations and carried away; cars become missiles (Less than 2 percent of tornadoes are in this category.)
F6	up to 300 mph	maximum	maximum tornado winds

Water on land turns into vapor, rises to form clouds, and comes back down as rain.

Water is continually going up into the sky and returning to Earth. Water from oceans, rivers, and other bodies of water is heated by the sun and evaporates. It goes into the air as water vapor, an invisible gas. Once it is high in the air, it cools into water droplets that form clouds.

When the air cannot hold the clouds of water droplets, it rains. Ice crystals fall from higher clouds. If the lower air near the ground is cool enough, the ice crystals will fall as snow. If the air is warmer, they will come down as rain or sleet. (Sleet is frozen or partly frozen rain.) Hail grows from ice crystals that start to fall but then spend more time in the cloud. While a tiny piece of ice is in the cloud, new layers of ice freeze on the water crystal until it grows to be a hard pellet. When it's heavy enough, the hail falls out of the cloud to Earth.

TUNE IN TO WEATHER!

Atmospheric pressure and relative humidity tell us things about the air that we cannot see. Turn on the news and listen to a weather forecast. The meteorologist, or weather person, mentions whether it will rain or not and the outside temperature to expect. Then the weather person announces the relative humidity, which is the amount of water vapor in the air compared to the amount of water the air can hold. If you hear the weather person say that the relative humidity is 100 percent, you know that the air is holding all the water it possibly can! If the relative humidity is 50 percent, the air is holding half of the water it can. Warm air can hold more vapor than cooler air. That's why it can get so humid when it's hot!

The meteorologist also gives the air pressure, which states how dense the air is. If the air is at a high pressure, it is more dense, meaning it is thicker than it is at lower pressures. Air moves from high-pressure areas to low-pressure areas.

HANDS ON!

MAKE RAIN: To make your own rain, first ask an adult to help you. Fill a pot halfway with water and cover it. Heat it on the stove and bring it to a boil. Depending on the pot, you may see steam seeping out of it. Now fill up a metal pie plate with ice cubes, take the pot cover off, and have an adult hold the ice-filled pie plate 2 to 3 inches over the pot using pot holders. You should see rain coming down from the pie plate!

37 | Clouds are made of water or ice.

When drops of water evaporate into the air, clouds form. But not all clouds are alike. Clouds come in many shades, shapes, and sizes. What a cloud looks like depends on how high it is, what the temperature in the sky is, and what form the water is in the cloud.

High clouds: High clouds are made of ice crystals. Cirrus clouds form at high altitudes and carry ice crystals. *Cirrus,* meaning "lock of hair" in Latin, lives up to its name. The clouds are thin white wisps. The fluffy white clouds that look like cotton patches are cirrocumulus clouds. Cirrostratus clouds are high and look like a big white, webbed sheet across the sky. These sheets of clouds often mean that it will rain or snow.

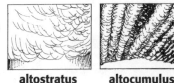

cirrus   cirrocumulus   cirrostratus

Middle clouds: Middle clouds are in lower altitudes and are made of water. Altostratus clouds are a bluish or grayish layer across the sky that bring rain. And altocumulus clouds are grayish white or gray small clumps of fluff.

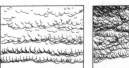

altostratus   altocumulus

Low clouds: Lower clouds sometimes contain supercooled water. These clouds mean bad weather is nearby. The small white, fluffy stratocumulus usually come right before or after precipitation. The nimbostratus are dark rain clouds, and the stratus are gray sheetlike clouds that can bring drizzle or snow.

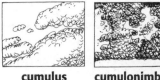

stratocumulus   nimbostratus

Vertical clouds: These clouds are like towers that contain supercold water above the freezing level. The cumulus are dome shaped and not too tall and are found lower in the sky. The cumulonimbus are large, appear high in the sky, and bring showers of rain, hail, thunder, and lightning.

cumulus   cumulonimbus

 **Every minute, about 600 lightning bolts strike the Earth.**

A lightning strike is a big spark of static electricity, similar to the tiny sparks of static that we experience when taking laundry out of a dryer or touching a television set. Of course, lightning works on a much bigger scale.

Lightning happens after a cloud becomes charged up. This means that the protons and electrons in the atoms

FUN FACT!

The temperature around lightning is six times hotter than the surface of the sun at about 54,000°F (almost 30,000°C). Lightning is usually about 3 or 4 miles long but is only about an inch across.

separate. If the top part of a cloud is positively charged, the protons are in the top part of the cloud and the electrons are in the lower part, creating a negative charge. Like a magnet sticking to a piece of steel, the opposite charges of protons and electrons naturally come together. Since the positive and negative charges always want to join, electrons suddenly jump to reunite with the protons in the cloud or on the ground. Lightning can occur from cloud to cloud or can come up from the ground to a cloud.

See pages 4–5 to read about atoms and page 14 to read about static electricity.

39 Mercury, Venus, Earth, Mars, Jupiter, Saturn, Uranus, Neptune, and Pluto are the nine planets in our solar system.

The solar system is made up of the nine planets and their moons. The system also includes the sun and all of the asteroids, meteors, and comets that revolve (orbit) around the sun.

All the planets orbit the sun in the same direction, and except for Pluto, orbit on the same plane. The farther a planet is from the sun, the longer it takes to orbit. For instance, it takes the Earth one year to orbit around the sun, but it takes Neptune 164.8 Earth years to make a single trip!

If you traveled to the asteroid belt between Mars and Jupiter, you would see thousands of asteroids (minor planets). Astronomers have spotted 8,319 asteroids, 5,848 of which have been named. (Asteroids can be found in other parts of the solar system, too.)

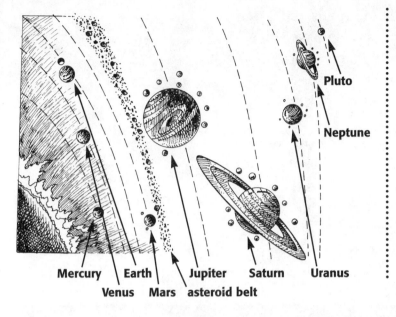

Mercury | Earth | Jupiter | Saturn | Uranus
Venus | Mars | asteroid belt

Pluto

Neptune

THOSE DIRTY COMETS

Made of ice, snow, and dust, comets are often called "dirty snowballs." When a comet gets close to the sun, its heat boils off a tail of dust and gas. One of the most famous is Halley's comet, which returns every 76 years.

WHAT'S THE DIFFERENCE BETWEEN A METEOR AND A METEORITE?

A small bit of rock or metal out in space, orbiting the sun, is called a meteoroid. If it collides with the Earth, it will be seen as a glowing spot of light, a meteor rushing across the sky. If it survives its fiery plunge through the air and lands on the ground, it is called a meteorite. Some meteorites are small chunks that have broken off asteroids. About 26,000 meteorites land on Earth a year. Most of them land in the oceans. They usually weigh about 3.5 ounces, about the weight of an apple.

meteorite

meteor   meteoroid

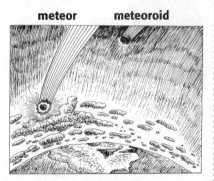

40 Planets are made of rock, liquids, and gas.

There are two kinds of planets. Mercury, Venus, Earth, and Mars are in the inner solar system and are "terrestrial" planets, meaning that they are rocky and dense. In the outer solar system, the planets Jupiter, Saturn, Uranus, and

Neptune are made mostly of liquids and gases. These gaseous planets also have rings around them. Saturn has the largest, brightest rings around it. The rings are not solid. They are made up of chunks of rock and frozen materials.

Saturn and its rings

Pluto, the outermost planet, is made mostly of ice and frozen gases and is the smallest of the planets. Even though it is called the outermost planet, it doesn't spend all of its time being the farthest planet from the sun. Planets orbit in elliptical (round or oval) paths, and Pluto orbits for part of the time inside Neptune's orbit.

The chart below shows that each planet has its own personality.

PLANET FACTS

Planet	Color from Earth	Diameter	Earth Time to Orbit Sun (Length of a Year)
Mercury	orange	3,031 miles	88 days
Venus	yellow	7,521 miles	225 days
Earth	blue & white	7,927 miles	365 days
Mars	red	4,197 miles	687 days
Jupiter	yellow	88,733 miles	12 Earth years
Saturn	yellow	74,600 miles	29 Earth years
Uranus	green	31,600 miles	84 Earth years
Neptune	yellow	30,200 miles	164.8 Earth years
Pluto	yellow	2,113 miles	249 Earth years

IS THERE LIFE IN OUTER SPACE?

SETI, the Search for Extraterrestrial Intelligence, listens for life from outer space with radio telescopes. The telescopes pick up radio wave signals from outer space. A constant stream of natural radio waves comes from space. Astronomers hope that some day the telescopes will pick up a special signal, or a message sent to Earth from other life-forms!

BRIEF Bio

NICOLAUS COPERNICUS (1473–1543):
Copernicus was a Polish astronomer who lived in Germany. He spent years studying the planets and was the first to show that the planets orbit around the sun. Most people at that time believed that Earth was the center of the universe and that the planets circled around it.

FUN FACT!

Venus, Uranus, and Pluto rotate on their own axes in the opposite direction from the other planets. This rotation is called retrograde.

41 The sun is a star and the largest object in our solar system.

The nearest star to us is the sun. Of all the materials in our solar system, including rock, gases, air, and water, 99.8 percent of it is the sun—that's how huge it is! And the sun, like all stars, is made up of hot gases, mostly hydrogen and helium. Stars are hotter than one can imagine. The sun's core is about 27,000,000°F. Our sun is a medium-sized star. It seems big because it is so close to Earth compared to other stars, a mere 93 million miles away! If you could take a jet to the sun going 600 miles an hour, it would take 17 years to reach.

Stars are born out of clouds of dust and gas and have lives just as we do. They start life as protostars. Gases and dust clump together and nuclear reactions start to happen inside the clump, causing it to shine. Stars live for different lengths of time, too. Some stars die after hundreds of billions of years, others, tens of millions. A star dies when it

WHY STARS TWINKLE

Stars look as if they blink on and off in the night sky. But stars themselves don't turn on and off. While the light from stars travels through the Earth's atmosphere, it has layers of gas and particles to get through before it reaches our eyes. By the time we see it, it appears to be twinkling. Stars seen above the atmosphere from spacecraft don't twinkle at all.

uses up all of its nuclear fuel. Sometimes when a massive star dies, a huge explosion occurs, called a supernova.

Supergiant stars are hundreds of times larger than our sun. Others are white dwarf stars that are dying and have shrunk down to planet size. Some dwarf stars are smaller than the Earth.

WHAT IS A LIGHT-YEAR?

It takes the sun's light just about 8 minutes to travel 93,000,000 miles to reach Earth. But it takes years for the light of other stars to get to Earth because they are so far away. A light-year is the distance that light can travel in 1 year, which is 5,913,000,000,000 miles. The sun is the closest star to Earth. The next closest stars are part of a triple star system: Alpha Centauri A, Alpha Centauri B, and Alpha Centauri C. Light from these stars takes 4 years to reach us, and thus, they are 4 light-years away.

42 | The moon, Earth's nearest neighbor, is about 239,000 miles from Earth.

Although the moon looks round, it is slightly egg shaped and is much smaller than Earth. It is a little more than one-fourth the size of Earth. And because

PLANETS AND THEIR MOONS

Planet	Number of Moons
Mercury	0
Venus	0
Earth	1
Mars	2
Jupiter	16
Saturn	18
Uranus	15
Neptune	8
Pluto	1

BRIEF Bio

GALILEO GALILEI (1564–1642): Galileo was an Italian scientist who did many experiments with gravity. He is known for dropping two things of different weight from the top of the leaning tower of Pisa and discovering that they landed at exactly the same time. He proved that objects fall at a rate of speed that increases the farther they fall. He was also one of the first to believe that the Earth moved around the sun and that the Earth was not the center of the universe.

the moon does not have an atmosphere to protect it, it can get as cold as -200°F at night or as hot as the boiling point of water during the day!

While planets in the solar system orbit the sun, moons travel around the planets. Our moon orbits Earth every 27.3 days, nearly a month.

43 The Earth orbits the sun as it rotates (spins) on its axis at 1,000 miles per hour.

The Earth spins, or rotates, on an axis and turns all the way around in 24 hours. Wherever you are during the day, Earth is facing the sun. At night the spot where you are faces away from the sun.

While the Earth is spinning on its axis, it is also traveling around the sun. Earth's trip around the sun is about 584 million miles long and takes 365.25 days. While the Earth orbits the sun, the moon orbits the Earth.

WHAT CAUSES THE SEASONS?

Some people think that the seasons happen because the whole Earth gets closer to the sun. They really occur because the Earth rotates on a tilted axis as we orbit around the sun. When the northern half of the Earth is tilted toward the sun (in June), the sun appears high in the sky and the daylight lasts much longer than the night. This is summer. Six months later, in December, the northern half of the Earth is tilted away from the sun. The sun then appears low in the sky and the night lasts longer than the daylight. This is winter.

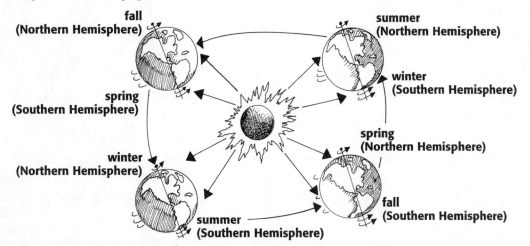

fall
(Northern Hemisphere)

summer
(Northern Hemisphere)

winter
(Southern Hemisphere)

spring
(Southern Hemisphere)

spring
(Northern Hemisphere)

winter
(Northern Hemisphere)

fall
(Southern Hemisphere)

summer
(Southern Hemisphere)

SOLAR ECLIPSES AND LUNAR ECLIPSES

A solar eclipse happens when the moon passes directly between the Earth and the sun. It blocks the sunlight to Earth and total darkness can happen in the middle of the day! A lunar eclipse occurs when the Earth is lined up between the sun and the moon. The moon shines by reflecting the sun's light, but during a lunar eclipse, Earth is in the way. There is no moonlight during a lunar eclipse.

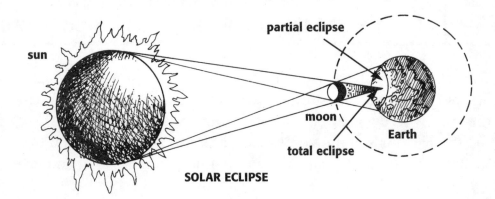

SOLAR ECLIPSE

44 There are 88 constellations, or groups of stars, in the sky.

When you see stars at night, you can connect some of them with imaginary lines to make figures. Early astronomers divided the night sky into constellations after objects, heroes, heroines, and beasts that the stars etched out. The naming of constellations started more than 5,000 years ago with the Sumerians (people of Iraq). Over time, the Babylonians and the Greeks used the same constellations. By the 4th century B.C., during the time of the ancient Greeks, there were 48 constellations. The Greeks added stories to go along with the constellations, and then the Romans added their own names and myths to the existing shapes in the sky. The Romans gave the constellations names in Latin, which today is the language of the official names of constellations. The last 40 constellations were added on in the last 400 years, and the names were not official until 1928.

HANDS ON!

<u>DO YOUR OWN STARGAZING!</u> It is best to go stargazing right after the sun goes down on a clear night. Since the Earth is rotating, if you find the Big Dipper in one place and look for it an hour later, it will be in a different place!

First, find the Big Dipper, a group of seven stars that seem to form a saucepan with a long handle. From there you should be able to find the North Star, the Little Dipper, Draco, Cassiopeia, and Perseus. Once you find the Big Dipper, look at the map (below) to find the other constellations. It may be hard to pick them out at first, because there are many other stars around the main stars you are looking for.

Here are some hints:

■ Once you find the Big Dipper, follow the two end stars in its bowl in a straight line to locate the North Star.

■ The North Star is very bright and is the end star of the Little Dipper's handle.

■ Draco's tail loops around the cup of the Little Dipper.

■ If you have found the North Star, the Big Dipper is on one side, and Cassiopeia is on the opposite side.

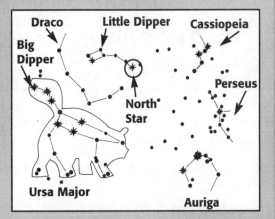

45 | Earth and our solar system are in the Milky Way galaxy.

A galaxy is made up of gas, dust, and billions of stars. Our galaxy, the Milky Way, looks like a hazy band of milky light across the sky, which is how it got its name. Galaxies come in all shapes and sizes but fit into two main categories: elliptical, which is round or oval, and spiral, which is like a big swirl. Irregular galaxies are those that take no spherical shape. The Milky Way is a spiral galaxy.

There are more stars in the universe than we can count. There are literally billions of galaxies, each one filled with stars. One galaxy that is next to ours is the Andromeda galaxy.

BRIEF Bio

EDWIN POWELL HUBBLE (1889–1953): The Hubble telescope is named for Edwin Hubble. He was an astronomer who studied galaxies and classified them as spiral, elliptical, or irregular. He also showed that our galaxy, the Milky Way, is just one of billions of other galaxies. One of his big discoveries is that the universe is expanding. With the help of telescopes, he noticed that galaxies around ours are getting farther and farther away from us.

46 The universe is expanding every minute.

The universe is made up of everything that exists, including at least a billion galaxies, each having billions of stars. Our solar system is like a tiny speck of dust in the universe, maybe even smaller! And the universe is getting bigger.

THE BIG BANG

Many scientists think the universe started with a huge explosion called the big bang. Scientists know that the universe is expanding and spreading out, so they try to think in reverse to figure out where the universe came from. Thinking of the expanding universe backward, everything would have been much closer together years ago— so close that at one time all the planets, stars, and galaxies were squeezed into a tiny pinpoint, smaller than an atom. The big bang theory is the idea that this pinpoint "universe" expanded and formed our universe today.

Scientists who believe in the big bang theory think the universe could be anywhere from 10 billion to 20 billion years old! The Earth is only an estimated 4 billion years old.

Take a deflated balloon and draw tiny stars all over it. Blow the balloon up. What happens? The stars spread out. If our universe is like the balloon, you can see how the stars get farther apart. The difference is that the balloon stops at a certain point. The universe keeps expanding!

 Fossils give us proof that life existed on Earth millions of years ago.

Paleontologists, scientists who study remains from past life, have found fossils. Fossils are plants and animals that have been preserved in rocks. They show us what kinds of life inhabited the Earth. Plants, footprints, feathers, bones, and shells can become fossils if the conditions are right.

Fossils can form in two ways. Fossils are created if rock forms around bone or shell or other hard materials like teeth that have not rotted away. The material gets buried under the surface, and the pressure of the ground on top helps to form a rock around the material over millions of years. Another type of fossil is made if rock materials shape around a life-form that completely decays. The space where the life-form has rotted away is filled in with minerals, creating a rock copy of what was once there.

FOSSIL FINDS

Archaeopteryx means "ancient wing," and it is the earliest known bird. Fossils preserving the Archaeopteryx date back to 147 million years ago and have been found in Germany and England. These fossils show that the bird had feathers, as well as many features similar to the dinosaurs. Because of these fossils, some scientists think birds are the closest living relatives to dinosaurs.

The first sign of life on Earth appeared about 4 billion years ago with a single cell.

Scientists are still trying to figure out how and when life started on Earth. Many scientists believe that life arose naturally, through chemical reactions that got more and more complex. They believe there was a time when the only life on Earth was one-celled bacteria in the form of blue-green algae. Microscopic fossils that are 3.4 billion years old have been found in Australia and South Africa.

The development of animals took place over a span of 570 million years.

When it was first born, Earth was covered with volcanoes and smoke. There was little or no oxygen, and—as far as scientists know—no plant or animal life existed. But fossils show that about a billion years later one-celled organisms lived on Earth. Fossils also show that there seems to be an order to how animals developed over millions of years. First there were one-celled animals, then multicelled animals, and later fish. Eventually life moved from water to land with amphibians, which gradually led to mammals. The time period chart on the opposite page shows the progression of life on Earth from one-celled creatures to today's living animals, including humans.

THE BURGESS SHALE

We don't have many fossils from the Precambrian period, but in Canada's Rocky Mountains the Burgess Shale fossils are like a photo album of life that existed 530 million years ago. With more than 13,000 fossils having been collected, Burgess Shale fossils are one of the largest groups of fossils in the world. Scientists have identified animals like Hallucigenia, which has seven pairs of spines!

TIME PERIODS (in shaded area, life was all in the oceans)

Precambrian before 570 million years ago	*The Precambrian period lasted about four million years and by its end, some animals were bigger than one cell, but they didn't have bones. They were somewhat like jellyfish.*
Cambrian 570–510 million years ago	*The Cambrian explosion marks the beginning of bigger-than-one-celled life on Earth. Animals on Earth went from simple one-celled organisms to animals with bodies and shells.*
Ordovician 510–439 million years ago	*During the Ordovician period, there were fishlike animals including worms, snails, and jellyfish. But these animals had no backbones or jawbones! This period was a time of ice ages on Earth.*
Silurian 439–409 million years ago	*First plants on land.*
Devonian 409–363 million years ago	*During the Devonian period amphibians started living on land. These animals looked a lot like fish with long tails. Today, amphibians still return to the water to lay their eggs.*
Carboniferous 363–290 million years ago	*Reptiles.*
Permian 290–245 million years ago	*Mass extinctions.*
Triassic 245–208 million years ago	*Reptiles or dinosaurs near the end of the period.*
Jurassic 208–146 million years ago	*Dinosaurs reigned.*
Cretaceous 146–65 million years ago	*Dinosaurs died out at the end of this period, and the first horse, the size of a dog, lived in this period.*
Tertiary 65–1.64 million years ago	*Mammals took over.*
Quaternary 1.64 million years ago to now	*Humans and the animal kingdom as known today.*

50 Dinosaurs dominated the Earth for 160 million years.

Dinosaurs are the biggest animals that ever lived on Earth. They are also one of the most successful animals, having ruled the Earth for 160 million years. (Humans have been here for only 2 million years.) Part of the dinosaurs' success was due to their ability to stand upright and move easily. Still, dinosaurs became extinct quickly at the end of the Cretaceous period. The dinosaurs may have died out because of a drastic change on Earth, such as a change in climate or a change in geography. Some scientists believe that a giant meteor hit the Earth and wiped the dinosaurs out. Whatever the big change was, the dinosaurs could not adapt quickly enough to survive.

FLYING REPTILES?

Closely related to dinosaurs, pterosaurs were reptiles that lived from the Triassic period until extinction in the Cretaceous period. They had wings made of skin (not feathers), some having a wingspan of 40 feet. Some types of pterosaurs weighed up to 220 pounds!

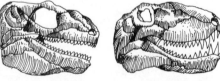

a plant eater   a meat eater

Scientists are able to study dinosaurs and learn how they lived from discovered fossils and bones. The many different types of dinosaurs can be split into two basic groups, depending on the structures of the pelvis: the reptile-hipped (saurischian) and the bird-hipped (ornithischian). The reptile-hipped dinosaurs were divided into the long-necked plant eaters called Apatosaurus and the meat eaters called Tyrannosaurus. The bird-hipped dinosaurs were herbivores and ate plants. From the teeth and jaw bone fossils that have been found, scientists can tell what they ate. Some meat eaters, such as the Dromaeosaurus, had long fingerlike claws and razor-sharp teeth. The bird-hipped dinosaurs had dull-edged teeth for slicing and grinding.

The largest dinosaur, the Brachiosaurus, was about 70 feet long and 46 feet high and weighed about 35 tons! The smallest, the Compsognathus, was about the size of a chicken!

To read more about herbivores, go to page 66.

51 Evolution is the change in all living things from generation to generation.

When scientists find fossils that show birds from millions of years ago looking more like dinosaurs than today's birds, how did it happen? Small, often unnoticeable, changes happen to animal species from generation to generation. The theory of evolution explains how these changes happen over time. These changes take place when animals become better at adapting to their surroundings. It is important to know that each individual animal does not change, but rather the group as a whole changes.

BRIEF Bio

CHARLES DARWIN (1809–1882): Darwin was a naturalist who spent most of his life observing plants and animals. He realized that fossils sometimes connect animals of the past to later animals. Fossils also show that life began with simpler forms. He came up with the theory of evolution: All present-day life-forms have gradually developed over millions of years from simpler life-forms. After years of research, he wrote the book Origin of Species, which introduces the idea that animals evolved through natural selection. However, Darwin was not the only one to think of evolution and natural selection. Alfred Wallace (1823–1913), also a naturalist, developed the theory around the same time.

52 The theory of evolution is based on natural selection, or survival of the fittest.

Survival of the fittest means that animals that are best suited to live in their environment have a better chance of surviving and reproducing. Some animals have an advantage over others. For example, if two deer live in the wild, the one that has longer legs and can run faster may have a better chance of surviving. More long-legged deer will survive and reproduce. The next generation inherits the traits of its parents and will be a generation of deer that mostly have longer legs. Over many generations, perhaps all of the deer would have longer legs. When a group of animals changes to have a better chance at surviving, the change is called adaptation.

WHAT PROOF IS THERE OF ADAPTATION AND EVOLUTION?

In the 1800s in England there was a group of moths called peppered moths. The wings of the moths had black and white patterns that blended in well with the light-colored lichen, a fungus on the tree bark in the area. Most of the moths had lighter colored patterns; only a small percentage of the moths were much darker. Because their coloring matched their surroundings, the moths were not noticed by predators. Over the years the pollution caused by factories became heavy, and the lichen on the trees started to get darker. The lighter moths became easy prey for birds. But the darker moths, even though there were fewer at the time, had an easier time surviving because they blended in so well with the trees. Many of the new offspring inherited the darker coloring because more of the parent moths carried this trait. Eventually, after many generations, the whole group of moths had become darker. In recent years the pollution in this area has been cut, and the moths are again adapting and becoming lighter.

 **Fossils show that today's mammals, while similar to their early ancestors, are very different in many ways.**

Fossils show the first horse to be the size of a cat. It also had four toes instead of hooves! It took 55 million years for the horse to evolve into the horses we see today. Early elephants, another example, were small and didn't have trunks. They had long noses and short tusks. Over time evolution has changed the horse, the elephant, and all mammals.

54 | Carbon is the most important element in living things.

Of the more than 100 natural elements on the Earth that combine to make up everything, only 25 are essential for life. Carbon is one element that keeps getting recycled between living and nonliving things. For example, carbon can be found in the molecule carbon dioxide in the atmosphere. This means that the element carbon is combined with another element. Plants take in carbon dioxide, break it down, and use it for energy. We eat plants and take in a form of carbon for energy. For instance, carbohydrates (which are listed on almost any food label) are made up of a carbon compound. Oils, fats, and proteins are also made up of carbon compounds. When our bodies break down the carbon compounds, a chemical reaction occurs and makes the energy we need to live. It is amazing to think that carbon is one of the most important elements in life, because in its pure form, carbon makes up the lead of a pencil or a diamond.

To read more about chemical reactions, go to page 8.

55 | All living things use energy, are made of cells, reproduce, and are able to adapt to their environment.

When you are alone, you may feel as if you are the only live being on Earth. But you are surrounded by life. Look around. Do you see any plants? Maybe there are some insects, or perhaps you have a pet. Even if you don't spot any of these life-forms, there are tiny living organisms around you that you cannot see! In fact, much of the Earth is covered with life. But what is it that determines that something has life? All things that are alive share common traits. That means that you have some things in common with even a small housefly. Some of the traits you share are:

- **Use energy.** You and the fly both use energy, even though you use energy for very different things, obviously, and you probably get energy from different foods.
- **Made from cells.** Cells are the building blocks of life. A blade of grass, the neighbor's dog, tiny organisms in water that you can't see, and you are all made up of cells.
- **Ability to reproduce.** You came from your parents. Someday you, too, may have children. The same is true for the fly. When living things make new living things, it is called reproduction.
- **Respond to changing environment.** When you're hot, you sweat. When you're cold, you move around to keep warm. You and your body know how to use energy and adjust to the environment to stay comfortable and to survive.

56 Every living thing starts out as one cell.

Living things are made up of cells, most of which are too small to be seen with the naked eye. Some creatures are just one cell, but most multicelled creatures (like you) start with a one-celled embryo, made up of an egg and a sperm. This cell contains all of

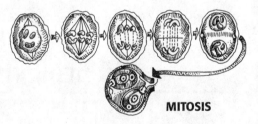

MITOSIS

the "instructions" to grow to what it is supposed to be. Before a cell splits, the instructions copy themselves. The one cell divides and the instructions are passed on. Then the two cells divide and so on. This process is called mitosis.

In order to do this, each microscopic cell has "machinery." Each cell has outer linings that allow certain substances in or out of the cell. And all cells (except the ones in bacteria) have mitochondria, tiny organelles that convert food and oxygen into energy. At

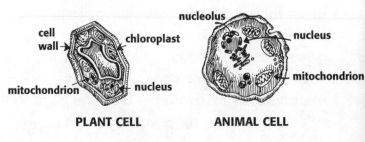

PLANT CELL

ANIMAL CELL

the center of most cells is a nucleus, which is where all of the instructions are.

Even though cells have all of these things in common, they can be very different from one another. For instance, the cells that make up your bones are much different from the cells that make up your muscles or your skin.

FUN FACT! All cells in the human body have a nucleus, except for red blood cells.

DIFFERENCES BETWEEN PLANT AND ANIMAL CELLS

Plant Cells	Animal Cells
have firm, cellulose cell walls	have no wall, but flexible membranes
a vacuole in the center	mitochondria to burn food, make energy
chlorophyll in the chloroplasts for photosynthesis	vary greatly in form

SHAPES AND SIZES OF CELLS

Individual cells are usually too small to be seen. Most animal cells are about 0.0004 inch across. They also come in different shapes; for instance, a nerve cell is long and slender, but a red blood cell is round.

In the nucleus of every cell is DNA, the chemical "instructions" that dictate what individual traits living things will have.

Deoxyribonucleic (dee-AHK-see-RYE-boh-new-KLEE-ik) acid is what DNA stands for. DNA is the chemical that makes up chromosomes and controls the traits of all living things. For example, it has the recipe for the color of your hair and eyes and whether you are a boy or a girl. In plant cells DNA contains the texture and shape of a plant leaf.

Chromosomes are passed on

FUN FACT! The DNA of a single human cell is about 6.5 feet long. If you think of the trillions of cells in your body, you can imagine how much DNA there is!

to you from your parents. You get exactly 23 chromosomes from your mother and 23 from your father. That is why children look like both of their parents. Two parents' chromosomes can be combined in so many ways that there is almost no chance of the same combination happening twice, unless they have identical twins. That's why sisters and brothers look similar, but not exactly alike.

BRIEF Bio

GREGOR MENDEL (1822–1884): Mendel was an Austrian monk who studied how traits are handed down from one generation to another. He carried out his study of genetics on pea plants. He would cross-pollinate different kinds of peas to see which characteristics were passed down. For example, he cross-pollinated peas with purple flowers with peas with white flowers. Because of Mendel's research, we now know how some traits are passed on from generation to generation in plants and animals.

Go to page 54 to read about cells.

BRIEF Bio

ROSALIND FRANKLIN (1920–1958): Rosalind Franklin was a scientist who studied DNA. She figured out that one way to get a better look at it was to crystallize it and then shoot X rays through the crystal. Her discovery helped scientists James Watson (1928–) and Francis Crick (1916–) figure out the structure of the DNA molecule in 1953. They figured out that when a cell divides, the ladder of DNA unzips down the middle. Unfortunately, Franklin was not fully acknowledged for her work until after her death.

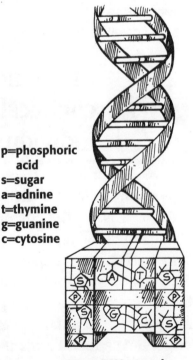

p=phosphoric acid
s=sugar
a=adnine
t=thymine
g=guanine
c=cytosine

a DNA strand

58 All living things fit into five kingdoms: Monera, Protista, Fungi, Plants, and Animals.

Carolus Linnaeus (1707–1778) was a naturalist who wanted to categorize all living things on Earth. He divided nature into two sections: plants and animals. Over time scientists have realized that more kingdoms are needed for classification. Now we have five kingdoms that all living things fit into: Monera (bacteria), Protista (single-celled organisms), Fungi (organisms that absorb their food from their surroundings), Plants, and Animals.

Linnaeus also came up with a two-part naming system for living things. He gave each a first name, for the individual, and a second name to show what family the life-form belonged to. He realized that each group could be categorized with other, bigger groups and came up with family, order, and class. His classification system is the basis for our current classification of living things.

Linnaeus used a universal language, Latin, to name everything in the system so that everyone in the world could benefit from it. For instance, *animalia* stands for animals of the animal kingdom; *insecta* stands for insects of the class of insects.

59 A seven-tiered classification system organizes all living things.

If you look at the chart below, you can see how each of the five kingdoms is broken down. After the kingdom comes the phylum, which separates animals based on their nerve cord. The class separates animals even more; for instance, mammals are a class, insects

FUN FACT! Reproduction happens only within the same species. You would never see a water beetle and a longhorn beetle reproduce.

are another. Order is more specific; for example, all beetles have their own order, even though they belong in the bigger class of insects. Family is a smaller group; for example, the longhorn beetles have their own family, separate from other types of beetles. Genus classifies things that are closely related. Species is the most specific.

HOW WE CLASSIFY:

HUMANS		TIGERS	
Kingdom	Animalia (animals)	**Kingdom**	Animalia
Phylum	Chordata (chordates, animals that have a single nerve cord)	**Phylum**	Chordata
Class	Mammalia (mammals, vertebrates that feed their young milk and have a coat of fur or hair)	**Class**	Mammalia
		Order	Carnivora (carnivores)
Order	Primates (includes gorillas, apes, and monkeys)	**Family**	Felidae (cats)
Family	Hominadae (standing upright)	**Genus**	Panthera (includes lions, tigers, leopards, and jaguars)
Genus	Homo		
Species	Sapiens	**Species**	Tigris (tiger)

 **Most living things in this world are one-celled creatures called protozoans.**

When you go swimming or visit a pond, you can see certain life-forms in the water. Maybe you see a frog, another person swimming, or some bugs floating on top of the water. The living organisms that you see are made up of millions of cells. Humans are made up of trillions of cells! But in that water, and in most any place you can think

FUN FACT!

More than 60,000 species of protozoans have been identified. About 24 of these live in humans.

of (including your body!), there are organisms that you cannot see. In fact, most of the world's living organisms can be seen only through a microscope. Scientists never knew about protozoans until microscopes were invented in the 1800s.

Are protozoans plants or animals? Some protozoans capture sunlight and photosynthesize to make food. Others capture and digest food, acting more like an animal than a plant! Because they act like both plants and animals, they are categorized in a kingdom of their own.

PUDDLE DWELLERS

Protozoans need water to live, but one special kind that adapts very well to its environment, the rotifer, mainly lives in puddles. If the puddle dries up, the rotifer can shrivel up and go into a sort of hibernation. When the water comes back, it comes to life!

Protozoans, the simplest form of life, can live almost anywhere as long as they are surrounded by moisture. Protozoans that live in animals are helpful because they can break down materials. One kind of protozoan that lives in termites helps the termite digest wood.

Most protozoans do not have digestive systems. Instead, they take in food by absorbing it through their membranes (the outer layers of the cells). The organisms have mitochondria, the parts of the cell that convert oxygen and food into energy. To move, some of these minute creatures have a tail called a flagellum, which whips around to propel them through water. Others have cilia, little oarlike hairs that move them around.

61 Fungus is neither plant nor animal but belongs to the fungal kingdom.

Fungi come in all sorts of shapes and textures. The most familiar and interesting-looking fungi are probably mushrooms found in the supermarket. Blue mold that grows on old bread is a

FUN FACT!

Orchids are plants that cannot survive without fungi. Some kinds of orchids are so dependent on fungi for nourishment that they don't grow roots.

A SYMBIOTIC RELATIONSHIP

Symbiosis occurs when two living things help each other survive. Some fungi live on tree roots. The fungi absorb nutrients from the soil and "share" some food with the roots of the tree. In return, the fungi get sugar back from the tree roots. In nature this happens between animals and also between plants.

fungus, too, as is the yeast used to make bread. Mold and mildew that grow in the bathroom are fungi, and rashes such as athletes' foot are fungi that grow on humans! Some fungi, such as spores, are single cells that float around in the air and are too small to see.

What makes a fungus different from a plant? Plants have roots and leaves and make food by photosynthesis. Most fungi absorb their food from their surroundings, like protists and bacteria. A fungus is a parasite—an organism that lives on and feeds off another organism called a host.

Fungi, like some mushrooms growing in the forest, can be poisonous, even deadly to humans. Other types of fungus are good for us, such as the mushrooms we buy in the store, which are a great source of vitamin C. And penicillin, a medicine that you may take when you have a virus, comes from a type of fungus.

WHAT IS LICHEN?

Lichen is a hard green plantlike growth that can be found on tree branches, rock surfaces, and even on cement. Lichen is a combination of a certain type of fungus and a certain type of alga. The algae use photosynthesis to produce carbohydrates, and the fungi extract the carbohydrates for food. The fungus protects the algal cell from getting too much sunlight.

62 Plants use the sun's energy to make their own food in a process called photosynthesis.

Clip the end of a plant off and stick it in water. After about a week, you'll notice that the plant is growing and has sprouted roots. But don't plants get nutrients from soil to survive? Plants do use nutrients from the soil, but unlike animals, which have to go out and find their food, plants make their own food with light, carbon dioxide, and water. Water travels up through the stem of a plant. Carbon dioxide is absorbed into the leaves of a plant through tiny pores called stomata. Sunlight shines down on the plant to give it energy to turn the water and carbon dioxide into food (sugars and starches), which makes plants grow. This process, called photosynthesis, takes place inside the leaves in tiny disks of chloroplasts.

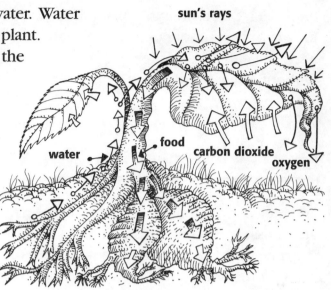

PHOTOSYNTHESIS

HANDS ON!

FIND STARCH IN PLANT LEAVES: Snip one leaf off a plant and put it in a dark place for at least a day. After the day has gone by, take the leaf out and put it on a saucer. Put a few drops of iodine on it and see if it changes to a blue-black. If the iodine stays orange, that means that the leaf has not been photosynthesizing. Snip a fresh leaf and put some iodine on it. What color is it? What is the difference?

 # Plants and humans depend on each other for the air they breathe.

While we breathe oxygen into our lungs to give us energy and help our bodies work properly, we exhale carbon dioxide. Plants do the opposite. They take in carbon dioxide to make sugars for food. This is part of the process of photosynthesis. After the carbon dioxide, sunlight, and water have been taken in by the plant, it releases oxygen. Plants are responsible for the oxygen in our air, and not only do we depend on them, but they need the carbon dioxide we exhale, too. Humans could not survive without oxygen, nor could plants survive without carbon dioxide.

64 Ferns and mosses have been around for 350 million years.

Some of the first plants on Earth were ferns and mosses. But the ferns and mosses during the time of the dinosaurs were quite different. They were giant—some mosses were 130 feet tall! That's hard to believe, because the mosses we see today are practically flat.

Many mosses and ferns do not produce seeds but instead produce spores, tiny cells that can start a new plant. On ferns the tiny brown spores can be found on the underside of the leaves. The spores are spread out by the wind and eventually grow into new plants.

MOSSES TAKE A NAP

Cryptobiosis is a state of suspended animation. Mosses, which are simple green plants, can dry out and seem to be dead. Once water is added, the moss comes back to life. This is how mosses can survive in dry weather.

IS A SEAWEED A PLANT?

Seaweeds have no flowers or leaves and also reproduce by spores. The California giant kelp, a type of seaweed, is the fastest growing plant on Earth. It can grow a foot in a day! Most seaweeds have a gas bladder that helps them float to the top of the ocean to get sunlight. This is important because seaweeds need the light for photosynthesis.

65 A seed is a package with all the ingredients needed to grow a plant.

All flowering plants produce seeds so that they can reproduce. The hard outer coating of a seed protects it from harsh weather or being destroyed by animals. What is special about a seed is that its inner layers have everything needed to sprout a new plant! Included is an embryo that later blooms into a plant. Also inside the seed is a layer of food to nourish the plant when it first sprouts.

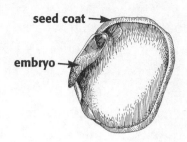

seed coat →

embryo →

HOW SEEDS GET AROUND

Seed dispersal gets seeds away from the parent plant in order to survive. Once seeds are produced by the parent plant, they need to be spread around so that they are not competing for the same food and sunlight. Often, animals will eat the fruits. The undigested seeds are excreted by the animal. If the seed falls into the earth, it can grow into a new plant. The seeds of maple, ash, and elm trees have wings. When they fall off a tree, they are propelled through the air and dispersed. Some seeds are in prickly burrs that get caught on animals and carried away to a new location. Others spread by falling into a river and floating downstream.

HANDS ON!

SEE SEEDS GROW: Seeds often grow underground where it is dark and moist, so most people never see seeds grow. But you can! Place a seed in a clear glass of very wet soil. Make sure the seed is against the glass. Keep it in a dark place and water it every other day. Each seed contains an internal food supply and doesn't need sunlight to nourish itself until it sprouts into a plant. Write down what you see so you can keep track of how fast certain types of plants grow. (Beans work really well for this experiment, but try corn and other seeds, too.)

Tomatoes, peanuts, and pea pods are fruits that come from flowers.

Flowers smell nice. They look good, too. But aside from making a nice decoration, flowers have an important job to do. Many flowers produce seeds and fruit that we eat. The seeds are made for reproduction of the plant. The fruit is a protective case that grows around a seed. Some foods that have been called vegetables are really fruits, such as tomatoes and squash. Some nuts, like hazelnuts and peanuts, are fruits, too.

Most flowers have male and female parts. The male part is the pollen-producing stamen. The female part is the pistil, a long tube that runs down to the flower's ovaries. In the ovaries are eggs. For the flower to be pollinated, the pollen needs to find its way down the pistil to the eggs. After pollination, fruit starts to grow.

FUN FACT!

The world's biggest flower is the rafflesia. This flower can grow up to 3 feet wide and can weigh up to 36 pounds!

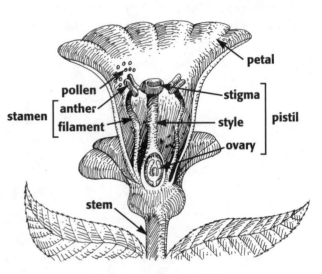

THE PARTS OF A FLOWER

HOW POLLEN GRAINS TAKE FLIGHT

Cross-pollination is one way that pollen grains get to the ovaries. Flowers can self-pollinate, but more often they are fertilized with the help of animals. Bees do a lot of pollinating! When a bee lands on a flower, it is looking for nectar and pollen to bring back to the hive. While the bee is tucking pollen (from the stamens) on the backs of her legs in "carrying pouches," some pollen sticks to her hairy body. She flies to

pollination

another flower to collect, and some of the pollen rubs off onto the stigma to find its way down to the eggs.

Wind can cross-pollinate, too. In fact, some plants rely on the wind to carry pollen grains to other plants to find their way down the stigma. It sounds impossible, but it's not. These types of plants produce millions of pollen grains. So even if some of them are lost in the wind, others will make it to the right place.

67 All trees are flowering plants and are either coniferous or deciduous.

Even though we talk about trees as if they are in a kingdom of their own, trees are flowering plants—just taller, usually. The flowers are not noticeable on all trees, such as the maple. Deciduous trees have broad leaves that fall off the trees at the end of each growing season, and conifers have needles that are lost slowly throughout the year. Pine needles are actually leaves. These sharp, slender leaves stay on the trees for 3 to 4 years.

deciduous   coniferous

A lot can be learned about the abilities of a tree by considering the trunk. Throughout a tree's life its

FUN FACT!

The redwood trees, which mainly grow in California, are the tallest plants living on Earth. The tallest living redwood still standing today measures over 365 feet tall. The biggest tree ever measured was an Australian eucalyptus at 435 feet tall.

trunk acts like a big straw. It is responsible for getting water from the tiny underground root hairs up to the top. This is amazing, given that many

HOW TO TELL THE AGE OF A TREE

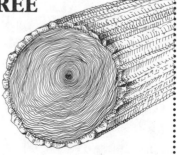

Trees grow out as well as up. Each year trees have a growth spurt in which a new layer is added to the outside of the trunk and underneath the bark. If you see a cut log, you can see the rings inside the bark. By counting the rings, you can tell how old the tree is. The widths of the rings indicate which years were good or bad growth seasons.

trees are taller than a two-story building! The water is transported to where the leaves are. With water and sunlight, leaves make food for the entire tree by photosynthesis. Once the food is made, the trunk transports the food from the leaves back down throughout the tree. The leaves also protect the tree from harsh weather.

 *To read more about photosynthesis, turn to page 60.*

WHY DO SOME LEAVES CHANGE COLOR?

Some leaves turn to beautiful shades of red, orange, and yellow in the fall. A leaf begins as green because of chlorophyll, the part of each leaf cell that is needed for photosynthesis. As days get shorter and cooler, chlorophyll slowly disintegrates. Other pigments that have been on the leaf all along begin to show through. Slowly the leaves turn from green to bright foliage colors. When the leaves are barely making food anymore (because the chlorophyll is nearly gone), minerals are transported from the leaves to the branches and tree trunk. The leaves fall off and the minerals are stored in the tree's tissues.

68 Carnivores are meat-eating animals and herbivores are plant-eating animals.

Birds swoop down to scoop fish out of water. Fish surface to eat insects. Insects chomp on plants. These are all parts of the food chain. All animals have to eat or they will die, and often they eat each other!

nature's food chain

Herbivores, animals that eat plants, are hunted by meat-eating carnivores. So, while grazing on grass or whatever greens the herbivores thrive on, they have to look out for carnivores. Omnivores are animals that eat both plants and meat. Insectivores, such as bats, moles, and shrews, eat mainly insects.

They have sharp teeth to bite through the hard shells of insects. Hunters, like the carnivores, are called predators, and the hunted are called prey.

Hunted animals have ways of trying to stay safe from their predators. Some travel in large groups and alert each other if a predator is in the area. The large groups make it hard for predators to focus on just one prey. These herds try to run fast enough to escape. Many animals rely more on camouflage, a way that animals blend in with their surroundings so well that they go unnoticed. The chameleon is famous for its ability to change color within minutes to blend in with its surroundings. Some rabbits become white in the winter to blend in with the snow, and many insects, when they stay perfectly still, look like twigs.

FUN FACT!

Porcupines have about 30,000 quills. Porcupines have a quill-covered tail that they can use to lash out at predators.

THAT TRICKY PREY

The possum plays dead when it is being stalked. The harmless viceroy butterfly has the same coloring as the North American monarch butterfly, which makes birds sick when they eat it. Birds stay away from the viceroys, thinking that they are monarchs.

Most of the world's animals are invertebrates.

Invertebrates are animals that do not have backbones. If you touch the middle of your back, you can feel your own hard, bumpy backbone. All mammals, birds, reptiles, fish, and amphibians have backbones. If this is true, how can most of the world's animals be invertebrates? Many invertebrates are too small to be seen with the naked eye. Some of them are made up of only one cell! Invertebrates range in size from microscopic one-celled creatures to the giant squid. A giant squid can be up to 60 feet long. Invertebrates include protozoans, sponges, cnidarians (ny-DAIR-ee-uhns), worms, mollusks, crustaceans and arachnids, insects, and echinoderms.

Protozoans. These single-celled creatures are considered to be the simplest form of invertebrate life. Some scientists are not convinced that they should be part of the animal kingdom. This is because some protozoans digest food like animals, but others act more like plants and photosynthesize their meal. Many scientists put them into a kingdom of their own, called Protista.

sponge

Sponges. These invertebrates live in the ocean. Sponges are strange animals because they look like plants. They have no head or digestive system and act like a bunch of single cells glued together. Most sponges live in warm, shallow seas and connect themselves to rocks, as moss on land would. They feed on plankton, tiny animals floating around in seawater.

Cnidarians. This group of invertebrate animals includes coral, jellyfish, and sea anemones. Sea anemones look like flowers made out of tentacles.

coral

worm

Flatworms, roundworms, and segmented worms. Segmented worms are found in gardens or in woods. Earthworms are a type of segmented worm. Flatworms and roundworms are often microscopic and in many cases parasitic (meaning that they live off another animal).

Mollusks. This group includes clams, scallops, squid, and snails. Even though a snail seems very different from an octopus, they are in the same group because of their body type. They are soft-bodied animals, many of which secrete a substance that hardens into a protective shell. In the octopus the shell is a small, barely noticeable plate.

squid

crab

Arthropods. All arthropods have pairs of jointed limbs, hard external skeletons, and jointed bodies. There are two categories of arthropods: the crustaceans and arachnids are one type; insects are the other. Barnacles, crabs, lobsters, and shrimp are crustaceans. Crustaceans usually have five pairs of appendages. Spiders are arachnids and have eight legs.

The other group of arthropods, insects, have six legs. Insects also have the advantage of wings that help them survive.

Echinoderms. Starfish, sea urchins, and sand dollars are echinoderms.

starfish

🌑 *Turn to page 58 to read about single-celled animals.*

70 Insects make up two-thirds of all the known animal species on Earth.

There is only one human species, but there are 800,000 different kinds of insects. Why so many? Because insects have been around for millions of years, and they are successful at surviving! Insects have certain advantages that help them survive. One advantage is mobility. Many insects have thin sheeted wings that help them travel over far

FUN FACT!

The stiff-winged dragonfly can fly over 18 miles in an hour!

distances. Wings help insects get around to find food, avoid predators, and, in some cases, migrate. Their six legs help them run quickly.

Insects have digestive tracts that can digest just about any kind of plant. Not only that, but insects eat meat, animal waste, and human blood! And, they're so small, they don't need much food.

Another advantage insects have is their senses. Most insects are covered

TRYING ON A NEW SKIN FOR SIZE

When spiders, crustaceans, and insects grow, they molt, which means that they shed their skin. If you have ever stepped on a bug, you probably heard a crunch or felt something break under your feet. The crunch was the insect's exoskeleton. All arthropods (a group that includes insects and spiders) have an exoskeleton. These hard outer coats of armor protect the animal's soft body. But exoskeletons do not grow with the animal. The arthropod sheds its exoskeleton in a process called molting. This process happens several times during an arthropod's growth stage. During molting, the arthropod is naked and vulnerable without its hard shell, but eventually a new and bigger one grows back.

with hairs that allow them to smell and taste. Next time a housefly lands on you, it's probably sniffing and tasting for food with its hair. To find their way around, many insects use tentacles. Certain types of ants use their tentacles to recognize whether other ants they run into are friend or foe. To see, insects have many lenses, unlike humans, who have one lens in each eye. Dragonflies have up to 30,000 different lenses!

Over three-fourths of all insects go through the four stages of complete metamorphosis.

Caterpillars turn into butterflies. Maggots turn into flies. Grubs turn into beetles. These changes happen through metamorphosis, a process in which winged insects go from egg to larva to pupa to adult. Most insects start out as an egg in the first stage. The egg hatches into a larva that looks nothing like the adult. Larva is the name of the first form the insect takes. The larvae are wormlike and often live

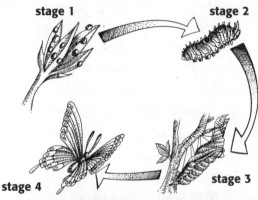

stage 1

stage 2

stage 4

stage 3

COMPLETE METAMORPHOSIS

in different surroundings than the adults. They have not yet developed compound eyes. The insect grows only during the larva stage, getting larger with every molt. When the growth is complete, it enters the third stage, called pupa. This is when many insects spin a covering called a cocoon. But some insects, like the caterpillars, are protected only by a thin membrane. During this stage the insect's body and organs change. The insect grows wings, the eyes develop, and a new flying insect emerges as an adult!

Not all insects go through complete metamorphosis. Some insects, like grasshoppers and cockroaches, go through incomplete metamorphosis. They hatch looking just like adults, only smaller. They do not go into a second or third stage of pupa but mature and grow into an adult.

 # Spiders are not insects but belong to their own group, arachnids.

Although spiders and insects are both arthropods, arachnids (the class spiders belong to) are quite different from insects. All arachnids have four pairs of legs and a body divided into two sections. Insects have six legs and a body divided into three parts. Spiders don't have wings or antennae, as insects do. They usually have six or eight pairs of eyes on top of their heads. Other arachnids are scorpions, daddy longlegs, and ticks.

FUN FACT!

The largest spider is the long-legged tarantula (also called the goliath bird-eating spider) of South America. It can have a leg span of more than 11 inches.

All spiders produce silk. The silk, made in a gland in the abdomen, comes out of the spider's body as a liquid silk and dries immediately. A newborn spider can spin a web as beautiful as an older spider. Spiders do not have to be taught how to spin, they know by instinct. Although spiders' webs are often beautiful, the purpose of webs is to catch prey. While sitting off to the side of the web, a spider can feel vibrations of prey entering the web. If the victim, an insect or

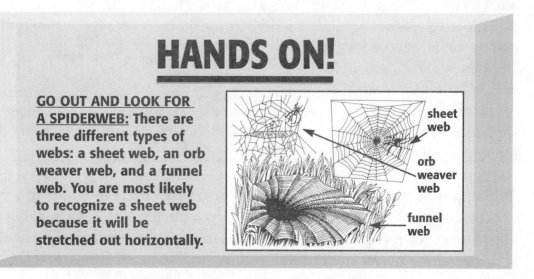

HANDS ON!

GO OUT AND LOOK FOR A SPIDERWEB: There are three different types of webs: a sheet web, an orb weaver web, and a funnel web. You are most likely to recognize a sheet web because it will be stretched out horizontally.

sheet web

orb weaver web

funnel web

another spider, gets stuck, the spider scurries out and poisons it. Once the prey is poisoned, the spider wraps it in silk to save for a later meal. Spiders eat insects by sucking out the liquid.

A few kinds of spiders find their food by hunting for it. The trap-door spider digs a little tunnel in the ground and makes a trapdoor on top of it out of silk. The spider hides under the door. When an insect walks over the silk door, the spider jumps out and grabs it.

WHAT A STRONG WEB SHE WEAVES

On average, it takes a spider 30 to 60 minutes to weave a web. Spiders have an oily coating on the bottom of their feet so they don't get stuck on their own webs. Spider silk is the strongest natural fiber, even stronger than Kevlar, the material used to make bulletproof vests. It's hard to tell this because the silk in webs is fine. Scientists are researching the best ways to make a synthetic (fake) spider's silk to use in manufacturing.

73 Honeybees, termites, ants, and some wasps live in organized colonies.

These insects divide up their work and take on distinct roles. Each insect knows what its job is and how to do it in order to make the colony run as best as it can. The honeybee, for example, has a whole system for running a hive smoothly. One queen bee does all of the reproducing for the hive. The rest of the honeybees

BRIEF Bio

KARL VON FRISCH (1886–1982):
Karl von Frisch, an Austrian scientist, studied animal behavior. He first discovered that bees do a dance to communicate with one another. After watching the bees closely for a number of years, he recognized the two types of dances that bees do, the "round dance" and the "waggle dance."

divide up their work according to their age. In the first 2 to 3 days of life, bees maintain the hive and clean the honeycomb cells. At 1 week old, honeybees feed the queen and the larvae, and at 2 weeks they start to make honey from the nectar brought in by older bees. Once the bees reach

3 weeks old, they become foragers, leaving the hive to find nectar to bring back that will become honey.

74 | Fish were the first animals with backbones.

A fish is a vertebrate, meaning it has a backbone. But fish have not always had backbones. Long before mammals, birds, reptiles, amphibians, and even fish existed on Earth, animals had few or no hard parts inside. They were like jellyfish. Then, over millions of years, fish evolved, but with no backbones and no jawbones. Millions of years later, fish with backbones evolved.

All fish have features in common, such as curved bodies that make it easy for them to glide, tails that propel them forward, and other fins to help with balance and steering. Fish are divided into two groups: those that have skeletons made of bone and those with skeletons made of cartilage. Cartilage is a softer material that we have in our noses, ears, and other places. The "cartilaginous" fish, such as sharks and rays, have a skeleton that is all cartilage. The only hard, calcified parts in their bodies are their teeth.

A SCALE OF GROWTH

A fish keeps the same number of scales throughout its life. As a fish grows, each scale gets bigger in size. As the scales grow, rings form, like rings on a tree. You can tell the age of a fish by looking at the number of rings on the scales. Not all fish (the catfish, for example) have scales.

75 | Frogs, toads, and salamanders are amphibians that live both in water and on land.

Amphibians evolved from fish about 350 million years ago. In fact, young amphibians usually resemble small fish and live the first part of their lives in the water only. Take, for example, tadpoles or polliwogs (baby frogs). Frogs, like many amphibians, lay their eggs in water. When frog eggs hatch, the tadpoles have gills like a fish and no legs, just a long tail that helps them swim. Legs start to grow and lungs develop. The gills slowly disappear and the tail starts to shrink. The tadpole becomes a frog over about 13 weeks. While frogs can live on both land and water, most live on land.

Amphibians are cold blooded, meaning their bodies have no way to regulate the temperature. Most of them live in the tropics, where it is warm year round, and those that live in cold climates hibernate for the winter. All amphibians shed their skin regularly. Their skin produces slimy or poisonous liquids that taste bad, making them undesirable or deadly to predators. Some amphibians rely on their skin for breathing. The lungless salamander absorbs oxygen through its skin from the water in which it lives.

76 Alligators, crocodiles, turtles, tortoises, lizards, and snakes are reptiles.

The first reptiles on Earth, the dinosaurs, are known for their massive size. Today, alligators and crocodiles are the largest reptiles roaming the Earth. Although some scientists suspect that the dinosaurs were warm blooded, today's reptiles are definitely cold blooded. For this reason, most of them live in the tropics, where it's warm year round.

Reptiles vary in their living habits. Many snakes live on land, and many turtles divide their time between both water and land. Most reptiles, however, lay their eggs on land. Even crocodiles and alligators, which spend most of their time in the water, lay their eggs on land.

Reptiles are covered by a thick, dry protective skin of scales. Snakes and lizards shed their skin, and the skin of crocodiles is continually worn away and replaced by a new layer underneath.

77 Birds have bodies that make it easy for them to stay up in the air.

As birds fly through the sky for hours, even full days, they seem to have an endless supply of energy. These warm-blooded animals have lightweight heads and sleek beaks instead of heavy teeth. Birds also have especially light skeletons. Many of their bones are like honeycombs on the inside and nearly hollow. The wing muscles of a bird can be up to 30 percent of its weight. If this were true of a 100-pound person, each arm would weigh about 15 pounds.

hollow wing bone

FUN FACT!

Hummingbirds flap their wings more than 70 times a second. Try flapping your arms up and down for a second. How many times can you do it?

Another main advantage to the bird is the wing structure and feathers. Wings are shaped like an arch, much like the wings of an airplane. This shape gives the bird lift and helps it stay up. Fold a piece of paper in half, then unfold it and lay it flat with the crease down. It will make an arch with a hollow underneath, like a bird's wing. Feathers help birds fly, and they act as an insulator by trapping heat near the skin. In hot weather, birds can fluff up their feathers to let body heat escape.

78 Some animals migrate—travel long distances for warmer climates and to find food.

Migrating animals are amazing, in that they somehow know where to go. While some animals travel short distances, others travel thousands of miles to get to their winter living area. Birds make these long trips to find warmer weather and a place where there are longer days to hunt for food. They return because there are better conditions for their young, such as available insects for feeding, less competition with other animals, and fewer predators. The arctic tern, a type of bird, spends warmer seasons on the arctic coast of Russia and migrates to the South Pole off Australia for the winter, covering 14,000 miles in each trip!

Birds are not the only animals that migrate. Monarch butterflies travel up to 2,000 miles from the U.S. Midwest to Mexico and back again. And some frogs hop less than a quarter of a mile from their winter home to their summer location.

THE MAGIC OF MAGNETITES

How do birds know which way to fly south for the winter? Scientists think that birds and other animals, such as sea turtles and honeybees, know which direction to travel in because of magnetites, little tiny magnets, in their brains. The magnetites work as a compass to tell the animal which way to go.

Mammals are warm blooded, have fur and hair, and most give birth to live babies.

Humans are mammals, along with dogs, elephants, bats, and hundreds of other species! Mammals always have fur or hair and a backbone. Because mammals are warm blooded, they have the ability to adjust to cold and hot weather. Along with their furry coverings, mammals can store up fat to burn

FUN FACT! Whales and dolphins, mammals of the sea, can feed on their mother's milk while underwater.

off when it is cold, and some mammals sweat to cool off when it gets hot. Cold-blooded animals cannot adjust to varying temperatures. A lizard caught in a snowstorm would probably freeze to death.

Also, all mammals have mammary glands, which produce milk for newborns. Most mammals give birth to fully developed newborns. When a human is going to have a baby, the mother normally grows the baby inside her for 9 months. Mammals that grow their young inside their bellies until it is time to give birth are called placental mammals. Two other types of mammals do not do this: marsupial mammals and monotremes. Marsupial mammals have pouches. At about 30 days, the inch-long newborn (not fully developed) crawls from the mother's birth canal to the pouch, where it can feed on its mother's milk. It lives in the pouch for 7 to 10 months. Some marsupials are kangaroos, possums, and wallabies.

Monotremes include only the duck-billed platypus, the spiny anteater, and the echidna. This group of mammals lay eggs! Like other mammals, monotremes produce milk to feed their young.

80 Humans, apes, monkeys, and lemurs all belong to the order called primates.

Primates have the most highly developed brains of all the mammals. Human beings have the advantage of verbal and written language to help us communicate with one another. Language also allows us to keep a record of what others have learned before us.

Like humans, primates have the advantage of having five fingers, including the opposable thumb. Try eating your cereal one morning without using your thumb. Or try writing with just your four fingers. It won't be as easy without that thumb! The thumb is called opposable because it can move toward the fingers, making it easy to grasp things.

FUN FACT!

Gorillas, a type of ape, are the largest living primates and can weigh more than 600 pounds. The smallest are a type of lemur, weighing only 1.6 to 3.2 ounces.

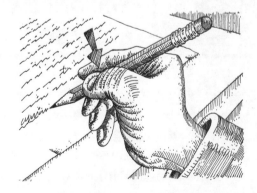

Humans and primates both have an opposable thumb.

Primates also have the advantage of binocular sight, allowing three-dimensional vision. Compare our eyes to other mammals' eyes. Consider the whale, a mammal that has an eye on each side of its head, giving it two completely different pictures. Out of each eye the whale sees a flat picture and cannot tell how far away things are. It would be dangerous for tree-traveling monkeys to be swinging through the trees without binocular vision!

BRIEF Bio

DIAN FOSSEY (1932–1985): Dian Fossey spent 19 years watching and living among a band of wild mountain gorillas. She followed the apes from afar at first. When she finally came close enough to them, she would drop to her knees so as not to scare them. The gorillas became used to Fossey. She spent much of her time trying to defend the gorillas against hunters. In 1985 Fossey was killed at her forest camp in Africa, but no one knows who was responsible for her death. Gorillas in the Mist was written by Dian Fossey in 1983 and later became a movie.

HOW ARE APES AND MONKEYS LIKE HUMANS?

Chimpanzees, which are a type of ape, are the most like humans. They kiss each other, hold hands, and pat each other on the back. In experiments with chimps, they have been able to learn over 300 symbols on a computer as well as sign language.

81 The brain receives 100 million signals every second from all over the body.

The brain is an organ that is made up of nerve cells—between 15 billion and 100 billion nerve cells! There are three main parts to the brain. Eighty percent of the brain is the cerebrum, which is made up of two smaller parts. The thalamus organizes sensory information coming into the brain, and the hypothalamus controls body temperature, heart rate, blood pressure, and hormones, as well as memory and senses. The brain stem is at the base of the brain. It controls body functions that we need to survive,

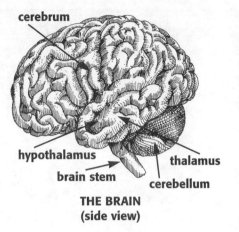

cerebrum

hypothalamus

brain stem

thalamus

cerebellum

**THE BRAIN
(side view)**

such as breathing, swallowing, and heart rate. The cerebellum monitors all of our movements, from helping us balance to drinking and running.

The brain has a distinct left side and a distinct right side. Both sides work together to do many things, but it is usually the left side that specializes in reasoning, language, and speech. The right side, the creative side, influences things like symbols, patterns, art, and music.

There are 206 bones in the human skeleton.

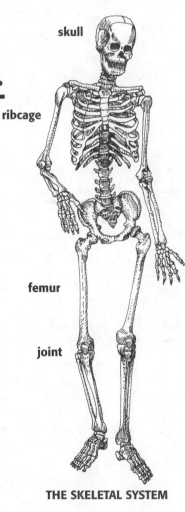

skull

ribcage

femur

joint

THE SKELETAL SYSTEM

While some animals have exoskeletons, hard outer shells, the skeleton of a mammal is on the inside of the body and grows as the animal grows. Human babies are born with a skeleton of 350 soft cartilage bones. Cartilage is a strong, flexible material that isn't as hard as calcified bone. As newborns grow, bones start to harden. By the end of the first year, 206 of the soft bones have turned

MEETING OF THE BONES

Joints, where bones meet, can be found at places where your body bends, such as your elbows, knees, and knuckles. Joints that move quite a bit are covered by cartilage and held together by ligaments (long stringy types of muscles). And they need to stay lubricated in order to move easily. A fluid keeps the joints oiled. Tendons are the tough fibers that attach bones to muscle.

into hard bones. Some bones stay as cartilage, such as the ones in the outer part of your ears and the one in your nose.

Bones are made up of two types of living cells. Osteoblasts produce new bone, and osteoclasts break down old bone. During growth, the osteoblasts are making much more new bone than the osteoclasts are dissolving tissue. When a person reaches about the age of 20 and stops growing, the osteoblasts and osteoclasts continue their jobs at an evened-out rate. As the bone cells are dissolved, they are continually replaced throughout an adult's life.

FUN FACT!

Teeth are harder than bones! Teeth, once we have our second set, do not keep growing as bones do. They are coated with enamel so they can last a lifetime.

SMALLEST AND BIGGEST BONES

The smallest bones are in the ear and are only one-tenth of an inch long. The biggest bone is the femur, the thigh bone. The skull seems like one big bone but is actually made up of 29 bones.

83 An adult body has more than 600 muscles.

Muscles work in pairs. When you walk or lift something, it isn't just one muscle at work, it's a team of them! Bend your elbow and bring your fist toward you. The muscles on the inside of your arm are contracting (getting shorter). The outside muscles are relaxed. Now straighten your arm. The outside ones contract and the inside ones relax. Muscles are made up of long stringy fibers and when they contract, you move. Skeletal muscles are connected to bones to help the bones move. Smooth muscles are found in the digestive tract and blood vessels. They contract more slowly than do skeletal muscles. Cardiac muscles are around the heart, helping to pump blood. The heart itself is a special kind of muscle, called myocardial muscle, and contains both smooth and skeletal muscle tissue.

Skeletal muscles are called voluntary muscles, which means that you think about moving and controlling them. For instance, when you walk, you first decide that you are going to walk, then your leg muscles move. The smooth muscles and the heart are called involuntary; they receive messages from the brain to work automatically without your thinking about it.

Your skin is your biggest organ.

The skin is made up of three layers. The outer layer of the skin is called the epidermis. This top layer has what are called pigments, which determine our skin color. The next layer is the dermis. This layer has blood vessels, nerve endings, the roots of hair, and glands. The third layer is made up of blood vessels, nerves, and cells that store fat. This inner layer keeps us warm, because fat can hold in body heat. Skin also plays a role in one of our main senses—touch. The many nerve endings in the skin help us to feel heat, cold, pain, and good feelings.

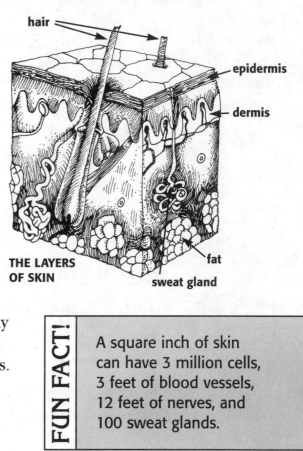

THE LAYERS OF SKIN

Skin protects us by reacting to temperature changes. We get goose bumps when we are cold because of tiny reactions at the root of each skin

FUN FACT!

A square inch of skin can have 3 million cells, 3 feet of blood vessels, 12 feet of nerves, and 100 sweat glands.

hair. This makes the hair stand up straight, causing tiny bumps. The hairs trap air, which acts as an insulator to keep us warm. Skin cools us off by sweating. Sweat comes from the sweat glands, most of which are in the armpits. There are 2.4 million sweat glands in the skin. If we didn't sweat, our bodies would keep getting hotter and hotter!

85

The nervous system is made up of the brain, the spinal cord, and all the nerves throughout the body.

The nervous system allows us to feel and react to things that we touch. When you touch something, receptors in your skin send messages to your spinal cord and up to your brain. Different receptors in your skin pick up different feelings. In other words, a certain kind of receptor feels heat and pain, yet another feels the cold, and another feels pressure. When the receptors feel these things, they send tiny electrical currents, which are nerve impulses, through billions of nerve fibers in the spinal cord and to the brain.

QUICK REFLEXES

Touching something hot causes an instant reaction! Why? When your receptors touch something dangerous, like a piping hot stove or something that causes pain, the nerve impulses don't take their usual path to the brain. They flash to a reflex center in the spinal cord, which causes you to jerk back without even thinking about it. Thanks to this shortcut in the nervous system, we are warned of pain and can better avoid it.

86

Smell and taste, two of our five senses, work together to send messages to the brain about what food tastes like.

Next time you sit down to eat, hold your nose. Can you still taste your food? Probably not, or at least not very well. The same thing happens when you have a cold. You cannot taste very well. This is because the sense of taste relies on the sense of smell. The other three senses are sight, touch, and hearing.

FUN FACT! You have about 30 million smell receptors in your nose. Humans can distinguish about 10,000 different smells!

    The tongue, covered with bumps, is used for tasting four basic flavors—sweet, sour, bitter, and salty. Each bump has sensory cells, or taste buds, in

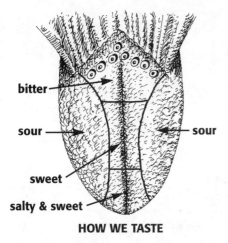

bitter

sour

sour

sweet

salty & sweet

HOW WE TASTE

FUN FACT!

The tongue is a muscle and an organ with four different types of taste buds. You have at least 10,000 taste buds on your tongue.

it. Taste buds, depending on where they are on the tongue, detect specific tastes.

The nose is a smelling organ that picks up smell from chemicals floating through the air. Once in the nostril, the chemicals are broken down by mucus they pass through in order to reach the hairlike cilia in the tiny nose organs. The messages are then sent to the brain to tell us what we're smelling.

87 The ear, used for hearing, has three parts and is shaped especially to capture sounds.

The outside of the ear is shaped to capture and funnel sounds into your ear. The sounds, which are vibrations, pass through the eardrum, a delicate, thin piece of tissue. The eardrum vibrates and passes the vibrations to a miniamplifier made up of bones in the inner ear. Once the vibrations are passed into the inner ear, a spiral tube filled with fluid triggers signals to a nerve that tells the brain what you are hearing.

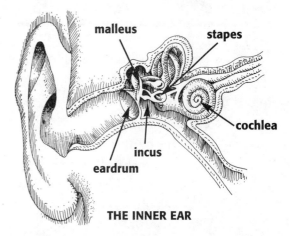

malleus

stapes

cochlea

incus

eardrum

THE INNER EAR

The inner ear also helps us stay balanced. Even when you close your eyes, you can stand up straight without falling down. This is because of a system of three canals in the inner ear. The canals are lined with hair cells and filled with a fluid. When you move your head, the fluid moves and the hair cells send messages to the brain, telling the body how to stay balanced. When you spin around in circles, the fluid and hair cells send messages. But when you stop, they keep sending messages, because they are still moving from having been shaken up. This is what makes you dizzy!

HANDS ON!

BALANCING ACT: You also balance when your body is around the center of gravity. Stand with your legs spread out. Now balance on one leg. You have just shifted your center of gravity. Try putting your right arm and foot against a wall. Now lift up your left leg. You'll be able to do it only if the center of gravity is over the right foot. The wall gets in the way.

The eyelid, pupil, retina, cones, and rods are all parts of the eye that allow us to see.

Our eyelids are like windshield wipers that keep the eyes clean and moist. They can also block out lights that are too bright. The pupil reacts to light as well. Look in the mirror and see the black pupil in the center of each eye. If a light is really bright, the pupil will get smaller. If it is dark, the pupil will get bigger. The cornea is a clear layer over the pupil that protects the eye. On the

FUN FACT! You blink 15,000 times in a day without even thinking about it.

inside of the pupil is a lens that takes in the "picture" of what you are looking at. The picture goes to the back of the eye, where the retina is. The retina is attached to the optic nerve, which sends signals that tell the brain how big or small the image is and how bright or dull the image is.

Inside the retina are rods and cones, cells that help the eye adjust to light and dark. The rods in your eyes give you black and white vision. When your eyes adjust to the dark, it takes a few minutes for your eyes to switch from cones to rods.

We see separately with each eye, but eyes work together to give us depth perception. Cover one eye and try to reach for something an arm's length away. You might miss without the use of the other eye! We also have what is called peripheral vision. Without looking to the side, you can still see out of the corner of your eye!

FUN FACT!

20/20 vision is a standard that means you can read from 20 feet away in a well-lit area.

89 The digestive system breaks down food, absorbs nutrients, and disposes of waste.

When you bite into something, your mouth waters. Actually, it fills with saliva, the liquid that starts to break down food the minute you bite into it. Your mouth can water if you smell food or think about it! Saliva also keeps your mouth wet, even when you're not eating.

The food that leaves your mouth has been chewed and broken down by the saliva. It travels down the esophagus, a long pipe, into your stomach. When the food gets to the stomach, strong acids in the

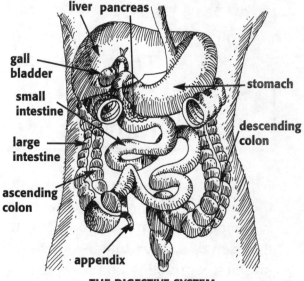

THE DIGESTIVE SYSTEM

stomach and more enzymes begin to break down protein. A layer of mucus coats the walls of the stomach so the acids do not bother the stomach itself. The food, now liquefied, makes its way to the small intestine.

Enzymes from the pancreas and bile from the liver flow into the small intestine to help break the food down even more. As that happens, nutrients are absorbed by the wall of the small intestine and go to the blood, which circulates throughout your body. By the time the food makes it to the end of the small intestine and into the

FUN FACT! The small intestine is 18 to 23 feet long. The large intestine is much shorter and wider than the small intestine.

large intestine, digestion is nearly finished. Only fiber, fats, water, and waste make it into the large intestine, where this material, called feces, eventually exits the body through the anus.

THE LIVER, THE BIGGEST INTERNAL ORGAN (THAT IS, INSIDE THE BODY)

The liver is like a big filter and has over 500 jobs to do. It stores vitamins and carbohydrates, makes special protein, and controls blood sugar levels. The liver filters out things that are bad for us, too. Nutrient-rich blood goes through this big filter system and then goes to the heart.

The respiratory system works with the heart to pump oxygen-rich blood throughout the body.

When we inhale, air is drawn through a windpipe to the lungs. This is not the same pipe that you swallow food with (the esophagus), although the two pipes are right next to each other. The lungs cannot move themselves, so breathing is done with the help of the diaphragm and chest muscles contracting and relaxing. Blood travels from the heart into the lungs to pick up oxygen, then goes back to the heart and into the bloodstream. Arteries carry the oxygen-rich blood from the lungs to all parts of the body. The oxygen is brought to cells that need it to turn food into energy.

91 The circulatory system is made up of the heart, arteries, and veins.

The heart is a special kind of muscle, called myocardial muscle. It is a combination of smooth muscle, the kind that helps the digestive system work, and skeletal muscles, the kind found in our arms and legs. It is involuntary and can change pace when needed. The heart is connected to the lungs so that blood can pump from the heart to the lungs to pick up oxygen.

Blood travels away from your heart all the way down to your toes and out to your fingertips in arteries. The blood returns to the heart through veins. Veins and arteries are not the same. Arteries are thicker and more elastic so they can contract to push the blood through. The veins, which return blood to the heart, have valves that are like trapdoors that

FUN FACT!
The heart beats about 3 billion times during a lifetime. At rest, the heart pumps 5 to 6 quarts of blood a minute through the circulatory system.

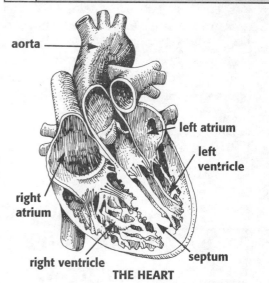

aorta

left atrium

left ventricle

right atrium

right ventricle

septum

THE HEART

HANDS ON!

TAKE YOUR PULSE: As the blood pumps through your arteries, it is pushed by the pump of the heart. There are places where you can find your pulse rate. Try placing two fingers on your wrist or on the side of your neck. You can also try your stomach, knee, or ankle. Time the beats for 15 seconds and then multiply the number by four. You should have a pulse rate somewhere between 70 and 100.

open only one way. The valves make sure that the blood goes in only one direction toward the heart. When blood gets back to the heart, it is full of carbon dioxide, which finds its way to the lungs and is exhaled.

BRIEF Bio

WILLIAM HARVEY (1578–1657): William Harvey, an English doctor, discovered how circulation works. Before Harvey's findings, people believed that blood moved through the body like the ocean tides—out and in, most likely through the same vessels. People also thought that air went through the blood vessels. Harvey dissected—cut apart—hearts, lungs, arteries, and veins to learn how the circulatory system works. When Harvey wrote his book, The Circulation of the Blood, in 1628, explaining how circulation really works, many people did not believe him.

WHAT COLOR IS BLOOD?

When blood leaves the heart with oxygen mixed into it, it is red. But as it passes through the arteries and loses oxygen, it becomes a darker color. If all of the oxygen were removed (which never completely happens), your blood would turn blue!

92 The endocrine system releases hormones into our blood to help us grow.

How does your body know when to grow? Or when to stop growing? What about burning energy? How does your body know to burn only a certain amount? Many things in the human body are controlled by hormones that are released from glands. Hormones are chemical messengers that are transported around the body through the bloodstream. The hormones regulate blood pressure, heart rate, growth, metabolism, and more! Glands are like chemical factories that produce the hormones. Eight main glands and hundreds of smaller glands, such as lymph nodes, make up the endocrine system.

The pituitary gland is most important because the hormones it releases tell the other glands what to do. The pituitary is about the size of a grape and is located in the brain. It produces more than two dozen hormones.

HOW DO HORMONES MAKE US GROW?

The pituitary gland produces at least five hormones that make us grow. One hormone that makes our bodies grow is called HGH, human growth hormone. HGH signals our bones to grow. Even though you do not keep getting taller throughout your life, HGH is produced for your whole life. When you stop growing, HGH still helps metabolize food.

 # Your immune system protects you from diseases.

The human body is under attack all the time. Our immune system protects us from things like bacteria (other than the bacteria that are supposed to be living in our body), protozoans, fungi, and viruses. When you get sick, your body tries to fight off whatever it is that has invaded it. Invaders can be a type of disease. Your immune system figures out what type of invader it is and responds by trying to kill it.

The immune system is made up of white blood cells. The white blood cells are produced in bone marrow and in the thymus, an organ in the upper chest. There are two main types of white blood cells, the T and the B cells. Some of the T cells signal other types of white blood cells to attack invaders. The B cells have antibodies in them. Antibodies are like weapons to fight off the invaders. The B cells receive signals from the T cells and are on patrol all the time. If they run into an invader, B cells release enough antibodies to smother the invader. The white cells are produced by lymph nodes, tiny pea-sized glands. Hundreds of lymph nodes are located throughout the body and are connected to one another by vessels.

The immune system protects the body but cannot fight off everything. Some invaders, like the AIDS disease, will try to beat the immune system no matter how strong it is. Other times, the immune system takes a few days to react to an invader, and the body becomes sick in the meantime. This is often why we catch colds.

94 There are two kinds of diseases: infectious and noninfectious.

There are thousands of diseases floating around, many of which are harmless, but others can be serious, even deadly. Diseases are either infectious or noninfectious. Infectious diseases can be caught from germs, another person, or from something in the environment. Some infectious diseases are measles, the common cold, and tuberculosis. Noninfectious diseases can be inherited. Examples of noninfectious diseases are diabetes and anemia.

BRIEF Bio

ELIZABETH BLACKWELL (1821–1910): Elizabeth Blackwell was the first female doctor in the United States. She was rejected by 29 medical schools because she was a female but was finally admitted to Geneva College in New York. Elizabeth had a hard time in medical school. As the only woman in her school studying to be a doctor, she was not taken seriously. After graduating, then practicing for a few years, she and her sister started a hospital in New York that eventually grew into a medical college and nursing school that accepted women.

All diseases attack the body, and many cannot be fought off by the immune system. There is no cure for the common head cold, an infectious disease caused by viruses. For illnesses caused by bacteria, if your doctor can figure out which bacterium has attacked your body, he or she can prescribe the right antibiotic medicine. An antibiotic is a drug that kills bacteria by attacking them or interfering with their ability to divide. (When bacteria get into your system, they start dividing and spreading!)

95 Sign and spoken languages were the first inventions of humans.

When you and your friends play a game, there are directions to guide you. Otherwise, how would you learn how to play? Someone could tell you how to play, but what if we didn't have language? Imagine what life would be like if we didn't have a way to communicate with each other. Think of going to school for a day and learning about history or math without language. It would be impossible!

Linguists, people who study languages, believe that humans have always had some way to communicate with one another. It may have started with signs, pictures, and even simple sounds. Now over 6,000 different languages exist, and it is believed that they have all grown out of one or just a few languages. Humans have also developed many ways to send and receive languages other than just by talking—telephones, letter writing, computers, and television, to name a few.

96 Stone tools from over 2 million years ago were humans' first technological development.

Technology is all of the things that shape our lives. The word *technology* is often used to describe high-tech concepts like the Internet, but technology

SOME HIGHLIGHTS OF TECHNOLOGY

Microscopes. Microscopes have helped scientists make breakthroughs in science because they allow them to see many things that could never be seen with the naked eye. The optical microscope has two lenses. It can magnify objects up to 1,500 times their normal size.

Spaceflight. Through technology, engineers have been able to build rocket engines, the only engines that can work in space, and computers needed to guide the space missions. Spacecraft must go 17,500 miles per hour to break free from the Earth's gravity.

Robots. A robot is any kind of machine that is controlled by computers to do a task. Robots can be machines in factories that do the same thing over and over, or they can be remote controlled. Many remote-controlled robots are built to do things that would be dangerous or even impossible for humans to do. Some have been built to explore volcanoes and even other planets, such as Mars!

can be as simple as moving something, whether it be
across the room or across the country. What
technology is also depends on where you live.
In the United States technology can mean
computers and televisions, while in another
country it can mean having telephones or
electricity for the first time ever.

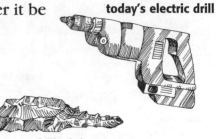

today's electric drill

a stone drill of the past

Technology has existed as long as
people have, but how do we know? Archaeologists have discovered stone
tools people made over 2 million years ago. From these tools, we know
that, even long ago, people were able to find better ways to cut, chop, or
bang, rather than use their bare hands.

97 | All the machines in the world can be reduced to six simple machines.

Try to envision the world without
wheels. How would we get
anywhere? Without wheels there
would be no cars, bikes, buses, or
trains! Wheels (with axles) are one of
the six simple machines that people
rely on. Another simple machine is
the screw. Practically everything is
held together by screws! Machines
make our lives easier in other ways,
too. The inclined plane, which is just
a sloping surface, allows us to slide a

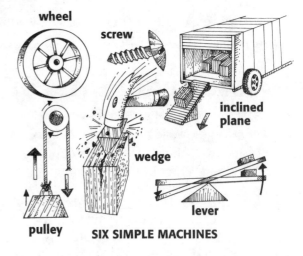

SIX SIMPLE MACHINES

load downward rather than carry it. A pulley, which is a cable that runs over
a wheel, helps us lift things that are too heavy. The wedge is shaped like a
wedge of cheese, and when hit with a hammer, it can split something open.
The sixth simple machine is the lever, which, like a seesaw, allows us to lift
something that is much too heavy to lift with our bare hands.

98 Steam engines powered trains, boats, and machines, changing industry immensely.

The horse and buggy could take people as far as they wanted to go before other modes of transportation came along, but it took a long time. Trains were the first engine-powered transport across the country, allowing people to travel great distances in less time. Trains also carried goods long distances, so people could buy and sell goods across the country. Steam engines changed the whole world of business, not just by powering trains. Before steam engines came along, most tools and machines were used by people, by hand. Steam engines started to be used in mills and factories and brought about a new age of industry.

The first steam-powered pump, which helped pump water out of coal mines, was built in 1698 by Thomas Savery of England. Thomas Newcomen, also of England, built the first steam engine. In 1763 inventor James Watt attempted to improve Newcomen's engine and invented the first railroad locomotive. Trains were not in the United States at that time, but by 1786 the first steam-powered boat was invented by John Fitch of New Jersey.

THE FIRST CAR

Cars also allowed people to travel more easily. Henry Ford is a name one thinks of in relation to the first cars, but Karl Benz, a German engineer, produced the first motorized tricycle in 1885. It wasn't long before Henry Ford's Model T came out in 1908. Cars at that time cost a lot of money, but Ford was the first to build a factory that could put together cars that could be sold at an affordable price.

Karl Benz, creator of the first car

99 Lightbulbs and electricity allow us to have longer days.

Think of all the things we do at night that could not be done without light or electricity—watching television, reading, playing video games.

Thanks to Thomas Edison (1847–1931) and his experiments with and inventions involving electricity, we are able to do these things. He did not invent electricity; the knowledge that electricity is created by traveling electrons had already been discovered. Edison developed ways to transport and capture the energy. He brought current electricity into homes, developed the first practical lightbulb, and invented the phonograph.

Even though electricity distributes energy quickly and to distant locations, the rural areas of many countries do not have electricity. When the sun goes down in these areas, the lights go off, except for candlelight or gas lamps.

 # Almost any information can be transformed into electrical signals, including a telephone call.

Telephones, designed to take advantage of electricity by sending electric currents through wires, were a huge breakthrough in communication. We live in a society today that depends on telephones to make communicating quick and easy. And telephones have come a long way. When they were first invented, there wasn't even a rotary dial. The first telephones went right to a switchboard operator, who would connect the lines and make the phone on the other end ring. Back then, telephone signals traveled as electric currents through wires. Now the signals can travel as light waves or radio waves. This is why we can talk to people across the world in seconds.

BRIEF Bio

BENJAMIN FRANKLIN (1706–1790): Benjamin Franklin was not the first person to think that lightning might be electric, but he was the first to propose putting up a tall metal pointed post to attract lightning from the sky. After seeing that this worked, Franklin did his famous kite experiment. Soon after learning about how electricity from lightning traveled through other objects, he invented the lightning rod to protect buildings from being struck by lightning.

Alexander Graham Bell (1847–1922) is known for inventing the phone, but Antonio Meucci, an Italian living in New York, also invented the phone at the same time. The first phone was patented in 1876.

WHY WAS THE TELEGRAPH IMPORTANT?

The telegraph changed the way we communicate. Samuel Morse (1791–1872) developed the Morse code, a way to spell out words with dots and dashes, for use on the telegraph. The telegraph sent electric signals over wires. Morse sent his first message from Washington, D.C., to Baltimore in 1844. This was one of the first uses of electricity.

The first computer took up a whole room.

Computers are used for everything these days, from air travel to medical technology to the tiny computers in cars. A computer is a machine that can do many tasks and can interpret information quickly, but computers can't think on their own. A computer uses algorithms, which are methods for solving problems. Most computers use digital codes, called binary codes, containing only two symbols, 1 and 0, to perform all operations. They are controlled by instructions called programs, which are written by humans.

Computers are part of sophisticated futuristic creations. Virtual reality combines imaging with computer technology so that users can experience what they are seeing as reality. Supercomputers are the most powerful computers and can do multiple calculations quickly. Scientists hope that supercomputers will be able to think like humans one day and make decisions in the same way we do.

EARLY COMPUTER WHIZZES

Ada Byron, Countess of Lovelace (1792–1871) was the first person to write a computer program. She wrote it for a machine that Charles Babbage (1792–1871) designed. Babbage designed the first mechanical computer but never built it, because his design was too complicated for the building equipment of the time. Grace Hopper (1906–1992) wrote the first program ever to be used, for the Mark 1, one of the first computers.

INDEX